The

Appearance

a crisis of perception

Guadalupe Press

Boerne, Texas

*For Information contact:
Guadalupe Press
Eron Howell
P.O. Box 865
Boerne, Texas 78006*

Starcke, Walter H.
The Third Appearance

ISBN 0-929845-07-2

*Book Layout, Cover Design and Original Painting
by
Kathwyn Eron Howell*

Also by Walter H. Starcke:

This Double Thread
The Ultimate Revolution
The Gospel of Relativity
Homesick for Heaven
It's All God

Upcoming Books:
Joel and I
The Daily Christ

Table of Contents

Part Two

The 3rd Appearance

a crisis of perception

by
Walter Starcke

Transition on October 25, 2011
90 years
May 3, 1921

My Uncle Gilbert lived humbly and quietly, Sidhartha fashion, in a ramshackle cottage on a small farm by a river outside of Seguin, Texas. During my early years of searching the world to find answers, I went to see him whenever I visited my family. In my youthful zeal, I bubbled over with what I had learned in some far-off monastery or in the esoteric books I was digging into. Although Uncle Gilbert is now long dead, I will always remember his best and still most difficult advice to follow: "Keep it simple."

The Foundation

We live in the most exciting, the most revolutionary, the most creative, the most challenging, and the most dangerous time the world has ever seen. Scientific genius combined with the arcane implications of mystical revelation has brought us to a crisis of perception, a decisive turning point where old structures must terminate or change.

As I approach my mid-eighties I find that my lifelong inability to exclude anything – any teaching, or any part of myself, or to capitulate to any one way of living, has turned out to be the very thing that now makes it possible for me to see that when we integrate the objective approach to life with the subjective approach we become the Third Appearance – *the incarnated presence of the divine.*

To some I may appear to be a spiritual anarchist out to destroy a number of religion's most sacrosanct superstitions, those previously thought to be prerequisites for spirituality. To others, what I have to say will be an avenue leading from past limitations into presently unbelievable new freedoms. Precisely because of my many years of trial and error, I have found and have personally demonstrated some of the necessary and very practical solutions that will take us there.

It is not my intention to either perpetuate or debunk traditional religions – Christianity, Buddhism, Hebraism, Islam, metaphysical or existential philosophies – but rather to explore and help initiate a new, non-sectarian "global myth" that will define the future.

The Mayan calendar, whose beginnings date back many thousands of years, ends on October 11, 2011, and similarly some futurists and intuitives have more recently announced that in just a few years the planetary cycle that the world has been undergoing for eons will end and be replaced by a new one. The new one will not be created by divine accident; we are no longer helpless victims of chance. For the first time, humankind is affecting its own evolution. Science, philosophy, and metaphysical mysticism are combining to give us creditable new insights that, when finally integrated into our consciousness, will make it possible for us to create whatever kind of world we desire for ourselves.

Most significantly, if we are to prosper we have to perceive something that has never been seen before. We must literally close the gap between our divinity and our humanity, between the visible and the invisible, between the subjective and the objective, and between consciousness and form. With the help of science it is possible for us to bring our abstract truths out of the clouds and down to earth. That is the only way that we can meet the challenges that we face at the less than absolute level of personal existence.

With lifestyle changes accelerating daily all of us, young and old alike, are forced to constantly reinvent ourselves in order to let go of obsolete values and inappropriate concepts that stand in the way of a necessary all-inclusive global approach. It's put-up-or-shut-up time. Either we will face this crisis of perception, or we will be swept along like a bunch of lemmings into a sea of confusion and darkness.

As inexcusable as some of the world wide, soul-shaking experiences of the past few years have been, it is no accident that the hole that was punched in the world's psyche on September 11, 2001, didn't happen until evolution was ready to move us collectively into a new dimension. Although the psychological, metaphysical, and spiritual principles that will make it possible for us to counter these critical times have been evolving over the years, until now we haven't been ready and able to take the next step. Most likely we have needed these disturbing times to push us into waking up. Finally there are enough of us who are able to absorb and demonstrate the truths that we have learned and intuited in our individual lives. Together we can form a critical mass, a heightened group consciousness, that will be powerful enough to "save the city."

It is not my intention to plunge into the forest of theology, or to try to back up my beliefs by hiding behind any particular religious tradition. Some of my examples will, of necessity, come from the symbols upon which our Western culture has been built – our Judeo-Christian background. It makes no difference if we have or have not agreed with the religions of the past, our society has been conditioned by those symbols. On the few occasions when I do refer to them, my purpose is to reinterpret them in a way that frees us from past moral and philosophical judgments.

Because the media constantly rehashes the dire events that are now happening in the world, if I attempt to counter them with the sound of metaphysical clichés, it will smack of hollow escapism or an attempt to offer a kind of temporary, spiritual anti-depressant. The best thing I can do right now is to take Uncle Gilbert's advice and be as simple, direct, and self-revealing as I can.

The first half of this book is dedicated to theory, with relatively few personal references or instructions that turn hypothesis into practice. The second half is far more personal and practical, as I implement my perceptions with techniques that have transformed my life in remarkable and undeniable ways.

At this point, we, and the world in general, are in a state of free fall. Objectively there isn't anything permanent for us to hang onto of a material or intellectual nature. We cannot find security in our bank accounts, our physical health, our mental storehouses, our governments, the teachings of the past, or anything else external to ourselves. If we curl up out of fear in free fall, we will spin helplessly out of control. On the other hand, if we do not panic, but instead stretch out our arms and trust that which we have within ourselves to protect us, we will not only glide down with a modicum of control, but we might enjoy the ride as well.

There is now incontrovertible evidence that mankind has just entered upon the greatest period of change the world has ever known. A fresh kind of life is starting. In the face of such an upheaval, actually shaken by it, no one can remain indifferent. No matter what reactions we may have to current events, we ought first to reaffirm a robust faith in the destiny of man. Mankind represents the culmination of the whole movement of matter and life, so far as it is within the range of our experience. Man, in these new perspectives, understand better his title to the sovereignty of the universe.

Pierre Teilhard de Chardin

Part One

Chapter 1

Science and Mysticism

The odd couple of the twenty-first century is the marriage of science and mysticism. Surprising as it may seem, because of this union we are now able to finally solve this crisis of perception and close the gap between imagination and fact, or the divine and the human.

When I began my conscious spiritual search some sixty years ago, I would never have believed that the day would come when science would accomplish something that organized religions had never been able to achieve. Today science is proving the existence of what we have commonly thought God to be, not just by theoretical speculation but also with empirically demonstrable material examples.

That fact doesn't make religious input or the mystical experience obsolete; instead it does exactly the opposite. Science is in the process of breaking down all material substances into what is called a "singularity," the single basic substance from which all life evolves. However, it takes mysticism – the experience of spiritual consciousness – to put the pieces back together in a way that will make living in the world like living in paradise. Exoteric science is telling us what material existence is made up of, but it takes esoteric spiritual wisdom to interpret and understand not only what constitutes life, but also how to live it.

Science is proving mystical truths at the objective or physical level that we have known subjectively for thousands of years, and in doing so science is making mysticism – the science of intuition – rational, practical, and undeniably necessary. Science and psychology are now telling us what is taking place in humanly identifiable terms; however, both our physical sciences and our mystical principles will remain half-truths that are independently unworkable unless we combine them.

Scientific research is opening a Pandora's box of incredible powers, where both the alarmists, those who predict the world's demise, and those with a positive attitude who believe that after a few hard-earned lessons we will turn our world into utopia, can plead their cases with conviction. While presenting both the negative and the positive possibilities of what may come about, I will quote a number of authorities in various scientific fields and will deal with some alarmingly disastrous predictions as well as some encouraging positive ones. With what would be to most people an inconceivable conjecture, I will offer an updated mystical explanation of who we are and our purpose for being here.

Whether we like it or not, science is driving us toward a material as well as a spiritual singularity, a time when technology and nature will have become one, and life as we currently know it will no longer exist. This singularity, where things born of nature and those born of man's runaway intelligence merge, is already taking place.

At present we are creating primarily bionic people, with artificial limbs and bodily functions that are controlled and set in motion by computer chips implanted in the human brain. Scientists have genetically altered mice so as to have human immune systems. We are transforming livestock by altering their genes, we have created an artificial womb capable of growing a fetus, and we are in the process of cloning human life.

Author James John Bell writes, "Researchers at the State University of New York Health Science Center at Brooklyn have turned a living rat into a radio-controlled automaton using three electrodes placed in the animal's brain. The animal can be remotely steered through an obstacle course, making it twist, turn, and jump on demand. It is most likely that in the future parents will want their offspring to be as close to perfection as gene-altering can make them."

Author Ray Kurzwell interprets this phenomenon as a "technological change so rapid and profound it could create a rupture in the very fabric of human history." Many futurists define singularity as a time when societal, scientific, and economic change will be so fast that from our present perspective we cannot even imagine what will happen. We can't close our eyes to the developments that are taking place, but we can translate them into their spiritual potential and become aware of how they relate to omnipotence.

An article by James Bell in the "Earth Island Journal" says, "There is no question that technological growth trends in science and industry are increasing exponentially. There is, however, a growing debate about what this runaway acceleration of ingenuity may bring. At this juncture, the world, as we have known it, will have gone extinct, and new definitions of 'life,' 'nature,' and 'human' will have to take hold."

Even now, IBM is working on a computer that can make a million billion calculations per second. Computer hardware will surpass human brainpower in a decade. Once we become machine-controlled the realm of the born – all that is nature, and the realm of the made, all that is humanly constructed – will become one.

San Diego University's Professor of Computer Science, Vernor Vinge, further elaborated on the danger of singularity, "We are on the edge of change comparable to the rise of human life on Earth. The precise cause of this change is the imminent creation by technology of entities with greater than human intelligence. We will have the technological means to create superhuman intelligence. Shortly after, the human era will end. From the human point of view this change will be a throwing away of all the previous rules, perhaps, in the blink of an eye, an exponential runaway beyond any hope of control. I think it is fair to call this event a singularity. It is a point where our old models must be discarded and a new reality rules." The London Times compared Vinge's statements to Einstein's letter to President Roosevelt warning of the danger of the nuclear bomb.

Alarmingly, the World Conservation Union and the International Botanical Congress has recently announced that a global mass extinction caused by our uncontrollable technology is already underway as a direct result of human ingenuity.

If that is not enough, Sun Microsystems' Chief Scientist, Bill Joy, gives credence to the coming singularity and warns that "Knowledge alone will enable mass destruction." He says that new, self-replicating technologies are being released into the environment that are nearly impossible to recall or control, and that the system of global capitalism, combined with our current rate of progress, gives the human race a 30 to 50 percent chance of becoming extinct when singularity is complete. He announced, "Unless things change we could be the last generation of humans." If by "humans" he means those who live by the first law of human nature – material survival rather than consideration for fellow man, compassion, and love – then I for one am all for it. After all, isn't that what Jesus and our other mystics have in mind when they exhort us to "die daily"?

If what these scientists predict comes about, we will be our own successors. There is no doubt that we will still be here, living on earth and inhabiting human personalities, but we will be super-humans – divinely inspired physical beings. We will be the first generation to arrive at spiritual singularity, a condition the mystics of all time have sought. Haven't they all said that our belief in separation from the One is an illusion, that there is but one all-inclusive being called God? When we combine spiritual singularity (an all-inclusive concept of divinity) with technological singularity, who knows, we might even become angelic humans! However, before we do, we must jettison the old concepts and superstitions about God and life which were suitable for their times, and wake up to a new realization of who we are today.

Spiritual Equivalent

*I*n contrast to the potentially negative possibilities attributed to the side effects of how we employ our technological advances, scientists continue to amaze us daily with life-enhancing and life-extending discoveries. They may not fully understand the spiritual, in lieu of religious implications of what they are offering us, but they are providing explicit and undeniable evidence that our physical presence and our spiritual consciousness relate and respond to each other. In doing so, they are proving the down-to-earth practicality of age-old mystical principles and the possibility of our closing the gap between the divine and the human. In plain language, science is proving to us that if we want to lead happy, healthy, and successful lives in the challenging days ahead, it is absolutely essential that we solve today's crisis of perception by adopting spiritual principles and healthy mental attitudes as the *modus operandi* of our lives.

Once we develop the capacity to subjectively experience what the physicists are proving objectively, we will not only pinpoint what has been causing much of the world's chaos today, but we will also discover how to effectively understand and cure the cause of all of our individual problems. When we become aware of the spiritual implications of what science is revealing materially, we will at last experience what the mystics in both the Occident and the orient have claimed to be true for centuries, that we individually have conscious access to an infinite divine intelligence that is the source and maintainer of all life.

Here are a few examples of how our scientists are leading us to the most life-altering discoveries since man has endeavored to figure out who and what he is. When I spoke at Virginia Beach in 2002 for the Edgar Cayce Foundation, the Association for Research and Enlightenment, I got further significant proof that we are now closing the gap between the material and the spiritual. Previously when I had spoken at their headquarters, I followed a physician, Depak Chopra. This particular year they had me follow Greg Braden, the brilliant young scientist, whose book, *The Isaiah Effect*, had just made a considerable impact.

In both cases, my inner guidance came through and told me what to say. Chopra comes from the Hindu tradition, and his scientific examples were interpreted through that cultural and spiritual context. I saw that I had to translate the universal nature of the same truths that Chopra touched on via my Western cultural and spiritual background, the Judeo-Christian tradition. On the other hand, Braden, in his talks, gave us a scientific viewpoint. To complete the picture, I followed with the metaphysical equivalent.

In Braden's lecture he showed how scientific research has

proved the effect of thought and emotion on our basic DNA. He explained that they had taken some saliva with its DNA from a donor, placed it under a measuring device, and then moved the donor into another part of the building. At exactly the same moment that the donor experienced an emotion, his DNA in the other room responded. To further substantiate the experience, they took a donor several hundred miles away from his DNA sample and the same thing happened. The second the donor felt an emotion, his distant DNA responded likewise.

Braden went on to explain that every cell in our bodies has intelligence. They communicate with each other, and through their research the scientists have found that when a person feels emotions such as anger, depression, or fear, the DNA in their cells – the double helix – tightens up and scrunches. But when a person feels peace, love, and contentment, that person's DNA loosens up and healing automatically takes place.

Without being knowledgeable about the physiological mechanics of how thought and emotion affect our bodies, metaphysics has been extolling the virtue of positive thinking ever since Norman Vincent Peale popularized *The Power Of Positive Thinking*. Until our recent scientific revelations, the only way we have had to back up our beliefs has been with a combination of faith and examples drawn from practical experience. Now we have empirical proof.

Because of these scientific revelations the students of the Unity teachings no longer have to take it on faith alone when they read how their founder, Myrtle Fillmore, cured herself of tuberculosis over a hundred years ago by talking to the cells of her body. She demonstrated that cells do have a kind of intelligence and that at some level we can communicate with them – exactly what the scientists are now proving.

Brayden also repeated that for the first time in recorded

history, through science, we have at our fingertips the ability to change our genetic code, alter the planet's weather, engineer new forms of life, clone old ones, and do those things that were formerly attributed to God. He added that the controversy over stem cell research and genetically altering foods implies that our technologies may have advanced beyond our understanding of how such knowledge affects our lives. Brayden rightly concluded that through technology we are extending our senses beyond the known universe, that the choices we make today will permanently affect the world's future, and that our technology has outpaced the wisdom with which we use it. He concludes that our technology must be married to purpose if we are to survive. That's where the mystics come in. Summed up in one word, they know the purpose – love.

I particularly agreed with Braden's statement that science breaks down the building blocks, but that it takes spiritual awareness to put them back together. In saying that, he puts the ball solidly in the court of those who have long claimed to believe in spiritual principles, not in religious dogma but in the power and existence of spirit.

Scientists have reached their level of expertise through countless years of study and dedication. Many of us have had our spiritual search at the forefront of our lives for an equal time. Now it is up to those of us who have arrived at a parallel spiritual conclusion to recognize that together we and the scientists can create the heaven this world is meant to be by closing the gap between science and the mystical experience.

Actually, the union of science and mysticism is a marriage that is being made in heaven. Scientists are proving the singularity of all material existence, and when we equate spiritual singularity with the physical presence of humankind, the oneness of spirit and matter will no longer be a fiction. The belief that either science or mysticism alone will be able to eliminate duality is destined to fail, but when they are combined as two dimensions of one reality a whole new way of life will be revealed.

When Braden repeated, a number of times, that there is an unknown web or energy field tying everything together which scientists are trying to discover, I wanted to run up to the platform and tell him, "I know what it is. That energy field is consciousness, or spirit."

Lipton's "What"

$\mathcal{A}$nother biologist whose work has recently produced scientific proof that corroborates a basic principle of metaphysics that I've intuited, gone public with, and tried to live by for years, is Dr.. Bruce Lipton, a Pathology Fellow at Stanford University's School of Medicine. His *The Biology of Perception* does more to close the gap between the spiritual and material and point out the necessity of our solving this crisis of perception as anything I've come across.

After a detailed explanation of what constitutes a cell, how it is formed, how it operates, how each cell performs the functions of sustenance and elimination, and examples of the intelligence contained in each, Lipton states that those who believe that their lives depend on the genes that they have inherited are wrong. Genes can't do anything until they are activated by proteins. In turn our environment – both our material and our mental environment – alters and affects our proteins. We inherit our environments, but it is our perception of the mental and physical environments in which we live that alters the molecular constitution of our proteins, which, in turn, affect our genes.

In fact, Lipton claims that our perceptions or beliefs can cause our genes to mutate. Mutation is not random as has been believed; we create mutations to cope with changing environments. That implies that in our drastically changing world, if necessary, we divine humans will be able to generate new capacities, even new body functions, to meet the exigencies of the times.

Lipton, similar to Brayden, also explained that when under stress our immune systems and growth processes literally shut down. When our TVs blast us with dire predictions of wars and threatening circumstances, how we perceive the news affects our DNA. To the degree that we fear or are concerned, our protein sequences alter, and if we believe or put negative energy into what we hear, we stop growing. A harmonious physical outcome brought on by a positive faith is not accidental. In other words, positive faith is not just a spiritual virtue – it is a physical necessity! Whatever we focus our intentions on we create through our perceptions. If our children can grow up understanding how significantly their perceptions affect their lives, they will avoid most of the pitfalls we have been heir to.

The Free Will Trigger

As the scientific building blocks began to add up, I ran into a fascinating explanation of how through free will our perceptions actually produce a physiological effect on us. The meaning and purpose of free will has always been a problem for me. In the absolute we do not have free will, because everything we have experienced in the past leads us up to and conditions the choices we make in the present. But as human beings we do have to use our free will, and it is somehow vitally important in designing the quality of our existence. That is why I deeply appreciate what I learned by struggling through a mind-challenging book that someone sent me entitled *Quantum Evolution* by Johnjoe McFadden, a professor of molecular genetics, at the University of Surrey, England.

As I read McFadden's book I plowed through the scientific mumbo-jumbo, attempting to digest the complex theories in the hope that at the end I would find something to substantiate and confirm my metaphysical intuition. The fact that the book said that we and our brains contain one-hundred-billion neurons and about a hundred-trillion non-nerve cells, each with its own intelligence, didn't help my intellectual juggling act. But when I finally reached the end of the book, my refusal to leave that mental jungle paid off with a sliver of confirmation.

The book ended up being more than just an explanation of the operation of quantum mechanics. It provided a physiological explanation of how the phenomenon of free will affects us materially and of its importance. After explaining the unbelievably complicated conscious and unconscious mental and physical steps that lead to an action, McFaddin said that there is something real in each of us that triggers every response. We can call it our will, or we can add it all together and call it the sum of our consciousness.

From the moment we get out of bed in the morning, until we lay our heads on the pillow at night, our wills are the process that sets the wheels in motion. The way our wills operate is how our minds move matter. Consciousness acts to modify or veto actions that are initiated unconsciously, but our will is similar to the arc in a light bulb that connects the positive and negative poles creating the light. Free will is the spiritual arc that connects consciousness to form and action.

McFadden explained, "Neuronal activity may precede

a conscious decision to act by three-to-four-hundred milliseconds; but there is still a gap of two hundred milliseconds between the awareness of a conscious intention to act and the initiation of the motor impulse." It is in this motor-lag period that consciousness has an influence on voluntary action. Free will is this two-hundred millisecond connecting arc (my word for the magic) that joins the spirit to the flesh. As human beings, we are responsible for that arc, which is our free will, and the quality inherent in what we "will" is the "word that becomes flesh." That is why our intention in life is so vitally important. Intention quantifies and qualifies the perceptions that through the will physically performs and directs our lives.

We live in what our current string theorists call parallel universes. The actions of our neurons exist simultaneously with non-physical consciousness. Ordinarily we cannot think two things at the same time, but because of our parallel existences and what Carl Jung called synchronicity, we can consciously experience separate levels that are not included in a single moment's thought. Free will is that arc joining the parallel existences, uniting spirit and matter, heaven and earth, or our perceptions and the forms they take.

– *The Bose-Einstein Condensate*

*N*ow for the most important and prophetic scientific revelation of all, the implications of which are almost impossible for us to imagine in our present mind-set. Everything I had been looking for since I began my spiritual search fell into place when I caught a glimpse of what Einstein was trying to prove when he came up with the Bose-Einstein Condensate.

The simplicity of Einstein's theory makes it almost impossible for it to be explained simply. Einstein, like the mystics who claimed that God and man are one, theorized that though there is no way we can know the particle (individual man) in terms of the wave (infinity), at one point they are one and the same. Individual particles or atoms can expand and merge into a single wave, like the particles of light in a laser beam, where they are at once one and equal. Unfortunately, at the end of his life Einstein felt he had failed, because he hadn't been able to prove his formula for that instant of unity that came to be known as the Bose-Einstein Condensate.

After Bose and Einstein announced their theory in 1924, many of the scientific fraternity of the time proclaimed that the theory was false and absolutely unprovable. It took until the new breed of scientists was able to put the necessary effort into testing Einstein's predictions that he was vindicated. In 1995 three American scientists from the American Research Institute were awarded the Nobel Peace Prize for doing what Einstein was unable to accomplish; they proved the Bose-Einstein theory. In doing so, they brought to light something that when fully developed will drastically change our lives and the world, both spiritually and materially, like nothing ever before. It may provide the only answer that can eliminate the present chaos in the world

The three scientists' dedication paid off when what turned out to be a speck of condensate consisting of thousands of super-cold atoms produced a single shadow that was recorded by a digital camera. They were awarded the prize for producing what was considered to be a bizarre state of matter in which individual atoms merged into a single wave-like entity. By actually producing such a substance, they proved that in reality the finite and the infinite are one and inherently the same.

Though it is beyond our pedestrian imaginations, this scientific break-through is enough for the scientific technicians to announce that in the future they will be able to produce usable technology that will make today's inventions look primitive. They tell us we will eventually be able to create a nana-technology enabling us to grow things as nature has, atom by atom, and be able to build super-intelligent computers that will be extensions of ourselves and give us dominion over our life experiences, turning them into something we can't even fantasize about today. When we, as spiritual scientists, prove that it is possible to close the gap between our divinity (the wave) and our humanity (the particle) and experience them as one, we will create a world with a different spiritual dimension as well. By transcending either-or thinking, we will become entirely new beings beyond time and space and find ourselves altogether freed from human limitation.

The catch is that in trying to understand the nature of this new dimension and how to live our lives until it fully evolves, we bump up against a dilemma similar to the one we faced in our high school science class. In school we found out that if we were to take ingredient A, with its component attributes, and mix it with ingredient B, with its components, we would end up with ingredient C, which in no way resembled either A or B. Our problem, then and now, is that humanly we can only think in terms of things that have already happened to us in the past. Thus we see future possibilities as no more than modifications or intensifications of what is familiar to us at present. When we, too, reach a spiritual condensate level where the human and divine are one, we will be transported into a whole presently unimaginable dimension – the spiritual condensate.

Einstein wasn't the only one probing the new dimension in the early twentieth century. In the same year that he and Bose came up with their theory the astronomer, Hubble, announced a similar and equally important revelation. By proving that our galaxy wasn't unique, Hubble merged the finite with the infinite in much the same fashion as Einstein's condensate.

I recently listened to a program on PBS television called *Scientific Friday*, at which time some of our top scientists of the day were interviewed. Their general conclusion was that we have now broken down the material elements of life to the point where there is nowhere further to go. From that, they project that the new frontier of science is the discovery of new dimensions – hopefully spiritual, scientific levels of condensate consciousness.

At the forefront of those who believe that the next step is for us to become aware of new dimensions are the scientists who have promulgated the currently evolving string theory. Along with theorizing that beyond a material explanation of life all of existence is made up of infinitely small strings of energy, the string theorists imply that we are on the edge of discovering the existence of parallel universes or new dimensions that exist simultaneously with our current sense of reality.

Those who believe that there is life after death, or the existence of invisible influences, may be intuiting one or more of these other dimensions. It is hard for us to imagine what those other dimensions consist of, but if we sense the possibility of their existence and open ourselves to it, we may discover that at brief moments we are already experiencing the spiritual condensate level of consciousness where our divinity and our humanity are interwoven.

If you are one of those who wants to go the theological Judeo-Christian route, you could make a case that when Jesus arrived at the ascension he experienced a different dimension. As the story goes, Jesus didn't fully reach that new level of consciousness until the very end – at his ascension. After the resurrection when he said, "Touch me not; for I have not yet ascended," he was saying that he hadn't yet reached the spiritual condensate breakthrough where the human and the divine were fully experienced as one. When he finally arrived, he did not ascend. We think of his ascension as though he took his earthly body with him to some other place, but that is not what happened. He transmuted to a different dimension, the dimension he called "My kingdom."

Because this next step of our evolution is only now being proved, it will take a while for us to demonstrate its potential in practically applicable ways that will affect our day-in-day-out lives. However, to the degree that we do understand the part our perceptions play and how they create our reality, we will find that our new discoveries will lead us into an unlimited ability to manifest the fulfillment of our material needs, into a level of consciousness that makes healings instantaneous, and toward the attainment of freedoms beyond anything from our past.

If you feel that reading about or contemplating Einstein's condensate experience or contemplating the possibility of your entering a new spiritual dimension to be a waste of your time, I ask you to reconsider. I have found that even though opening myself to incredible new possibilities seems impractical, doing so activates my consciousness in a way that allows my intuition to bring forth new understanding and reduced limitations. It also helps me to be more tolerant with the presence of my personal confusions when they occur. In our evolution we are caught between the past and the yet-to-be-understood new dimension. Confusion lessens when we consciously let it reveal itself.

Contemplating the possibility of experiencing new dimensions of consciousness helps us to understand why sometimes we feel, perhaps ominously because of current political and social situations, that imminent changes are about to dramatically affect and alter our lives. Knowing that what we are feeling is not just personal, but that it is the result of the process of our collective spiritual maturation, dwarfs our petty personal problems and helps us continue to stretch toward the highest spiritual realization that we are capable of attaining. It helps us to reinterpret our humanity in a positive way, to be willing and able to respond more openly and successfully at our interpersonal and social levels, and, above all, it helps us to be patient and to trust the evolution of consciousness that is at work in both our personal lives and in the scientific discoveries that are taking place.

Chapter 2

The Consciousness Century

*M*y previous thumbnail sketches of ground-breaking scientific discoveries are certainly not adequate to endorse or support my thesis of the Third Appearance. At best, they are linear or third-dimensional explanations. In order to bring us to an other than intellectual assumption, we have to enter fourth-dimensional cluster thinking where, like a juggler, we keep a number of concepts in the air at once. The glue that holds all my conclusions together requires that we have a mutual understanding of, and a personal experience of, the word "consciousness."

We live, move, and exist in a sea of consciousness, an infinite ocean of levels of awareness manifesting as our individual lives. Without the realization that consciousness is operating behind all the situations and appearances that are taking place in our lives, it is impossible to close the gap between the visible and invisible and experience the spiritual condensate.

Einstein spent the later years of his life trying to find a way to dispute the universe that the quantum physicists were suggesting to him. His relativity approach dealt with the infinite "all," while quantum mechanics centered on the infinitesimally "small." Though his condensate theory actually proved the mathematical logic that pointed to the universe being non-local, which means both "here" and "there" at the same time, he couldn't agree. What he contested was the theory that a non-local universe meant that it is possible for a seemingly unrelated action in one place to affect other situations at other locations and that there are hidden variables embedded in reality that control the outcome of the physical world. Action at a distance means that there really is a connection among all parts of the universe similar to Greg Brayden's DNA tests that showed simultaneous DNA responses at a distance. That connecting link is consciousness.

A non-local universe means that everything each of us does affects everyone else, not just spiritually, but also materially. Though quantum physics is fundamentally a seemingly objective approach that deals with material outcomes, I believe that at a profound level the most spiritual books being written today are those coming from our quantum physicists. They both show and affirm how invisible spirit, or consciousness, visibly affects our lives.

In every culture there is a concept of the existence of a creator or source of creation. In the West we call the creator God. In India they call it Brahma. Our quantum physicists have come up with a new name for it – consciousness. They have concluded that consciousness is the creator, and are substantiating their claim by proving that everything that exists is invisible consciousness appearing visibly in or as form. In other words, form is a projection of consciousness.

Quantum physics states that an object cannot manifest itself in ordinary space-time reality until we observe it as an object, which means that for something to exist it has to be in consciousness. Though consciousness always has a location, a quantum object can be at more than one place at a time. When consciousness is no longer present, whatever form it symbolized ceases to exist. Once we perceive ourselves as being the presence of consciousness, we will understand that we have within us the same power or source of creativity that we have attributed to God.

Pierre Teilhard de Chardin, a priest and a scientist, was one of the first to close the gap between consciousness and form and recognize its spiritual implication. As a paleontologist and one of the discoverers of Peking Man, he proposed that all of creation has consciousness – that even a rock represents a dense and low-grade state of consciousness. Whenever consciousness is removed from a thing, it ceases to exist.

The only thing that can possibly be omnipresent is consciousness or spirit. Obviously, finite form can't be everywhere. Since all intelligence is an expression of consciousness, omniscience is consciousness. Everything that exists is first created through, as, and out of consciousness; therefore, consciousness is the only power or creator there is.

Recently, I received a letter asking me to define the word consciousness in a simple enough way that an eight-year-old could understand. In attempting to do so I turned to *Webster's New Twentieth Century Dictionary.* It wasn't any help, because it still offered a definition that was carried over from the nineteenth century. It left out the experiential nature of consciousness and labeled it a noun meaning "Awareness, knowledge of what is happening." Webster's did try to define the recently invented phrase, "consciousness-raising." However, it continued by saying that consciousness-raising is a noun, meaning "The process of seeking to increase awareness of one's role in connection with problems of modern life."

My answer to the eight-year-old was that "your consciousness is an invisible picture of who you are. It is made up of all that you think, feel, care about, all that you like or dislike. It includes all the things you remember, those you have forgotten, and those of which you have yet to become aware. Your consciousness is what causes you to make the decisions you make."

The word "consciousness" has become so much a part of our daily lives that it is hard for us to believe that just a hundred years ago the word was seldom used. When it was used, it was interpreted simply to mean mental or conscious awareness, rather than what we now think of as our total awareness – our unconscious, our subconscious, and our infinite super or latent divine consciousness. Unless we are referring to a particular aspect of consciousness, the word summarizes all the multi-dimensional aspects of our being rolled up into one.

If someone were to ask me to select a single word that would sum up the most important subject that our evolution brought us to in the twentieth century, it would have to be "consciousness." That is the century when we became aware of the reality and importance of consciousness. By the latter part of that century, phrases such as "becoming conscious beings," "conscious evolution," or that there is a "collective consciousness," were common usage in futurist, metaphysical, psychological, and scientific jargon.

What takes place in and as our consciousness has not only become the focal point of our psychology and our mental sciences, but it has also become the cornerstone of quantum physics, which is in the process of proving that consciousness is the ultimate cause and reality of all that exists.

Our acceptance of consciousness as an invisible reality represents a significant shift in how we evaluate life. There are two basic approaches to the way we function as human beings; both are necessary and both are equally valuable. We either judge life objectively by relating to visible material appearances, or subjectively, in terms of invisible values and purposes. Together they represent our consciousness. We can arrive objectively, step-by-step, to an awareness of the subjective truths symbolized by what we see, or we can become aware of how the subjective nature of a thing or situation is arrived at and has created its objectified presence. In other words, we can go from effect to cause or from cause to effect. We can see a situation and from there backtrack and know what caused it to appear, or we can discern the presence of a state of consciousness and know what will result from it.

Whether what appears to us as material reality actually exists or whether it is similar to the image projected onto a movie screen is another matter. Until now the objective way of evaluating life has predominantly assumed top priority, while the subjective, symbolic, or spiritual importance of what we see has been of secondary importance. Once we accept or perceive the creative nature of consciousness, our priorities begin to shift. Making war, dropping bombs on innocent people, using economic pressure to get results, or promoting acts of terrorism are examples of groups and nations giving precedence to an objective approach. When the subjective approach becomes primary the conditions that lead to terrorism, such as poverty, a lack of education, or limited opportunity will be eliminated and there will be no more wars.

A hundred years ago if I had said what I am going to say now, I would have been sent to an asylum. In today's more tolerant world I can openly announce the truth; I don't see any people. Rather, I see states and stages of consciousness manifesting itself in forms. Of course, I see bodies, but the invisible subjective character, vibration, or consciousness I experience in or as a person is more relevant to me than the objective form I see with my eyes. I see bodies as metaphors of the consciousness they symbolize. Viewed from that perspective, there was *no* Jesus, Buddha, Shakespeare, Einstein, or any of the scientists I have previously referred to. There has always been *One* evolving universal consciousness, and when each additional aspect of consciousness came into human awareness it was labeled by or identified with the personality through which it manifested itself.

How often have you said to yourself, "I should have followed my first impression; it's almost always right"? At those times you first sensed the presence of the state of consciousness that was present, but then you let your mind, which was loaded with previous judgments, take over. You may have talked yourself out of your gift of intuitive truth.

Though we are not always aware of it, everything we do is an expression of our consciousness. You wouldn't be reading this book if it were not in your consciousness to be doing it. It was in my consciousness to write it, but it was your own consciousness that drew the concepts included in this book into your awareness. If there weren't a reason for what is being said to enter the catalogue of your conscious awareness, it wouldn't be happening.

Our crisis of perception, and the effect that thought has on matter, is a classical example of how science is proving the existence of consciousness, or spirit. In doing so, they have shown us that the mystics have been right when they have said that we are not living a life of time or space, but as spirit, which knows no time, no distance, and no boundaries. The way in which our own consciousness unfolds dictates the quality of our physical and human experience. When our scientists discover the nature of consciousness, they will realize that they have found what most people think God to be.

In 1954 the author Joel Goldsmith, whose mystical message was ahead of its time, not only prophetically voiced what scientists are now proving, but also clearly gave us the spiritual principle that is now being scientifically revealed. He said, "Consciousness always has a form. If consciousness did not have form, it would be non-existent. The moment consciousness has existence, it exists as something, and that something must be a form of reality. The reality of being, whether of mind, body, or purse, is consciousness unfolding and disclosing itself individually, on the level of our respective here and now." In other words, we are not just states of consciousness; we are consciousness itself.

In his original, unedited lectures entitled *Consciousness Unfolding*, Goldsmith went on to say that by expressing states of consciousness we affect our physical lives. He wrote, "Health is not a condition of body, but a condition of consciousness. Wealth is not a condition of purse, but of consciousness. And when you learn to close your eyes and think in terms of I AM consciousness, then as consciousness, I am what I am conscious of experiencing. Do not separate 'mind' and 'body.' Do not separate consciousness and body. Do not separate yourself in any way. Do not separate any part of your experience from consciousness. Learn to close the eyes and begin to realize your life as consciousness." The premise is that when you know your life as consciousness appearing in the form of your body, your body will then be what it was intended to be – a tool or instrument for you to use in the pursuit of your life's purpose. As such, your perceptions dictate the conditions of your body.

The mystical principle that the science of perception proves to us is that through a transformation of our own consciousness and how we perceive life, we no longer need to be victims of circumstance. When we are faced with what appear to be possibly dire circumstances, if we can *perceive* a positive outcome we create conditions that separate us from apparent probability. By subjectively becoming aware of the consciousness of a situation before taking action at the objective level, we can be masters of our own destinies.

I am not denigrating the importance of our physical bodies, but when we begin to be consciously aware of ourselves as being primarily consciousness with bodies rather than the other way around, we begin to have dominion over the way our bodies react. And once we begin to interpret personal, national, and international issues in terms of the consciousness they represent, we will know better how to take effective actions to help change the consciousness when necessary.

In 1914, Max Plank, the father of quantum mechanics, claimed not only that consciousness or mind was the source of all creation, but that matter, as such, does not exist. That was exactly what the founder of Christian Science, Mary Baker Eddy, announced well over a hundred years ago in her Scientific Statement of Being – "There is no life, truth, intelligence, nor substance in matter. All is infinite Mind (consciousness) and its infinite manifestation…" That principle became the underlying foundation of the whole metaphysical (mind over matter) movement, a movement based primarily on a subjective experience of life that, in turn, would manifest objectively as a more healthy and harmonious way of living.

This shift in awareness from an objective way of looking at life toward a subjective approach may sound speculative, but in order to understand the evolution of our spiritual consciousness and to discover how this non-material viewpoint can affect our day-to-day existence, we have to become aware of a whole new way of perceiving ourselves. That is why we are facing a personal crisis of perception.

Becoming aware of ourselves as consciousness rather than bodies may sound far-fetched and of little consequence; however, I will share a personal example that proved it to me.

In the early nineteen nineties, on my ranch in the Texas Hill Country, winter was just ending and horseback riding season was imminent. Our horses hadn't been ridden for some time, but nevertheless, about ten of us decided to ride out and go down a narrow path into a nearby canyon. Halfway down the narrow rocky path, a lady's horse balked and refused to go further. My friend became anxious; so I helped her off her horse and put her on mine. By this time all the horses were getting restless; therefore, I immediately jumped up on her horse without taking the time to calm him down. The horse reared up, lost his footing, and fell over backward on top of me. After he rolled off me I couldn't move, so we all knew that it was serious. An ambulance was called and I was taken to a hospital in San Antonio where they X-rayed me and found that several ribs had been broken and both sides of my pelvic bone had been severely fractured.

Throughout this part of the experience I felt as though I was observing what was happening to me, rather than participating in it. My only thought was, "What am I going to learn out of this?" Once I was in my hospital room that feeling continued, and I went through the whole experience without taking any painkillers, drugs, or sleeping pills. How? I didn't need any painkillers or drugs because I literally hovered over my body and didn't feel any pain. I found that if I didn't move I didn't hurt. It was as though I was watching me rather than being me. When I sought an understanding of what was taking place my memory flashed back to something that began many years ago.

Back in the late 1940s I had read about remarkable physical feats that Hindu yogis could perform, how they could stop their hearts from beating, be buried alive and come back, and even tele-transport themselves. I started studying everything I could get my hands on about astral travel, out-of-body experiences, and other such phenomenon – some phony, some real. Eventually, I had a couple of remarkable experiences where I seemed to be in two places at once, or witnessed things happen without being physically present. At that point my inner guidance said, "Now don't play around with that any more. You have learned the principle involved, and further experiments will be both a waste of time and an ego trip – a phenomenal rather than a spiritual experience." So I dropped that pursuit and never thought of it again until 30 years later. Lying in that hospital bed without consciously thinking of what I had learned in the past, it took over.

I can explain in a sentence how an out-of-body experience such as mine can take place, though I can't always actually repeat it myself just by wanting to. In direct ratio that you are aware of yourself as consciousness with a body rather than a body with consciousness, you are not limited to a body. Consciousness knows no time or space and is free to travel, whereas material sense is bound by both time and space. Once we begin to experience ourselves as consciousness we are on our way and will eventually be able to take that awareness to extraordinary lengths. In the second half of this book I will discuss how to condition consciousness in order to attain that level of awareness.

Where We Live

*B*efore going on, I want to pause a minute and offer you a simple test to help you understand to what degree you perceive yourself as consciousness. Ask yourself, "Where do I live?" If the first thing that pops into your mind is that you live in a particular city, a house, or a geographical location, that thought indicates that you are still primarily viewing who you are and where you live objectively.

To the degree that you identify yourself with a location, you still think you are an object rather than being consciousness. You still believe that you are what you see in the mirror, rather than the life force or consciousness that is seeing through your eyes, digesting your food, or breathing your breath. It would be all right for you to continue to see yourself and where you live objectively, except that your survival may one day depend on your ability to experience yourself as informed consciousness rather than as a physical object. Remember that consciousness is not limited to time or space. Therefore, as consciousness you are not limited to material restrictions and you will enter a whole new way of life. It is when your material circumstances seem most chaotic that you are facing your crisis of perception.

Once we stop thinking of ourselves as only physical bodies, we will automatically see appearances subjectively as symbolizing the consciousness that created them. We will know that if we want to change the form, we must change our consciousness through how we perceive things. We must change our perceptions. When we are asked where we live our answer will be that we do not live in man-made cities or buildings, but rather that we live in cities of ideas and beliefs.

The cities of ideas that we exist in won't have physical boundaries. Our consciousness-cities will be composed of and populated by those who have the same values, the same ideas and the same consciousness that we individually inhabit. Certainly we will still have material lodgings with E-mail and street addresses, but the boundaries of our cities – our city limits – will be defined by the consciousness we live in.

Those who lived in the cities of the past were brought together by objective goals, by mutual material desires and for protection. The idea cities of tomorrow will be constructed from the consciousness of those who are drawn together for the survival of their souls, not of their bodies or material possessions.

In similar fashion, our families won't be made up of those with whom we share a physical heritage. Our families will be those among us who share the same consciousness and values that we do. No matter where we are physically, when something takes place that is detrimental to our shared belief system, we will consciously feel it.

An article that appeared in the *Austin American-Statesman* in 2002 by Bill Bishop and Mark Lisheron, equated the building of our present-day "idea" cities with the game of Monopoly. They said, "Cities expanded because their land was cheap, their workers skilled or plentiful, and because they were on river or trade routes. They grew with Reading Railroads and Boardwalks, and by adding houses and hotels, but the game is changing. The board's been jostled, the pieces scattered." Their conclusion was that in the future people will believe that the ideas and creativity that inhabits the houses and hotels will define the new social order. Most importantly, people will move away from the cultural norms and traditions that have defined our country for the past two hundred years.

Bishop and Lisheron also point out that Americans are leaving traditional organizations in droves. The Rotarians, Kiwanis, PTA, and the Red Cross are all losing members – their numbers are down by half since 1965. This dwindling social capital is accompanied by a decrease in financial capital those institutions have traditionally depended on for their survival.

Robert Cushing, a retired University of Texas social

scientist professor, made a study of fifty states and a hundred major cities, and came up with a startling observation: American cities generally high in traditional measures of social capital were lower in technology development, lower in income, and lower in population growth. He claimed that where many people attended church or were active in religious organizations, economic growth was the slowest. Those cities strong in faith-based institutions were also weaker in the development of technology and new patents.

High-technology cities, such as Austin, Seattle, and San Francisco, were the exact opposite. They had a lower percentage of people going to church regularly, fewer joiners, fewer volunteers, and fewer people involved in traditional politics. Those cities where technologic and scientific ideas were abundantly produced were fast growing and prosperous. They were populated with people of diverse backgrounds, interests, races, and spiritual interests who joined boycotts and protests, signed petitions, and participated in reform movements. More importantly, they put their money where their ideas were.

Another professor, Richard Florida, who authored *The Rise of the Creative Class,* says that these new idea people don't move to traditional cities with civic clubs and bowling leagues, but, rather, they head in the other direction. He writes, "Communities that once attracted people now repel them. People want diversity, low entry barriers, and the ability to be themselves." The people in these cities tend to be more optimistic and self-confident than residents in more traditional American communities. What's more, these cities are the best at promoting economic growth. "Diversity and its running mate, tolerance, appear to be the source of economic power in the cities of ideas. The economy isn't building itself on the institutions and culture of 50 to 80 years ago. Joiners aren't driving the economy in these cities of ideas with close ties to particular organizations. Interactions among people who do not look alike or think alike are the driving force to economic success now."

What does that tell us about the effect of consciousness? It says that churches prospered in the past because they were places of revolutionary ideas, and for them to be successful now, they must come up with completely new ideas, or at least a new packaging of old ideas. It tells us that people are listening, that people now know who they are and are ready to stand on their own. The institutions and relationships that were responsible for building the materialistic concept we call the American dream are fading out. Social structures and organizations that were dominant until the last couple of decades now fail to manifest prosperity. In their place we will reverse the previous order where material accomplishment was primary, and in doing so our organizations of ideas will prosper.

Unless there is a corollary between our ideas and the quality of spirit or consciousness inherent in them, our cities of ideas will also self-destruct in time. Today the script is being written by every professional and intellectual pursuit, telling us that we are in a critical stage of our consciousness evolution, if not revolution. The values we individually perceive will decide the outcome.

20th *Century Evolution*

My attempts to define and describe consciousness will remain abstract exercises unless I can substantiate them by offering several objective examples. There are a number of outstanding events that took place in the twentieth century that can help us understand how consciousness evolved during that time. Having lived through four-fifths of that century, and having been personally affected by many of the changes as they took place makes it possible for me to see how our understanding of consciousness developed. I am going to point out three significant examples that illustrate the evolution of consciousness during the twentieth century. These, among many others, represent one seamless process that is still taking place today.

1. The Death of God

$\mathcal{A}$t the beginning of the twentieth century, there were three men in particular who voiced a heretical concept with such profound spiritual implications that the Orthodox Church adamantly rejected them all. Nietzsche, Dostoevsky, and Freud introduced the beginnings of a revolutionary shift in consciousness and were universally reviled for it. Because revelation is never easy, those who initiate progress often pay a heavy personal price – Nietzsche and Dostoevsky went insane at the end of their lives, and Freud became a drug addict. Like the man, Jesus, they confronted the established order with a new concept of God. Those who were at that time founding the metaphysical movement, both in America and elsewhere, were simultaneously reinterpreting the traditional meaning of God. But by putting it in a religious context, although controversial, it was less disturbing to the reigning establishment.

Nietzsche, Dostoevsky, and Freud, each in his own way, announced that God was dead. This concept was widely publicized and discussed a half-century later in the 1950s when a book with that title was published. Their work resulted in two important things. They laid the groundwork so that the divinity of individual man could be consciously realized, and through the "death of God" they created a new religion for many – the deification of science. Before the twentieth century, religion denied the omnipotence of science, and until scientists like Einstein and Plank came along, science denied the power of spiritual perception. While agreeing that there is an order or design for life, Nietzsche, Dostoevsky, and Freud were simply saying that the objective or basically materialistic concept of God as a super-being sitting on a cloud judging and punishing humankind does not exist.

Nietzsche was the most maligned of those who were exposing the narrowness of a father/God concept. His saying that God is dead led most people, in particular theologians, to think that he believed that nothing of a divine or spiritual nature existed; whereas he was actually centering divinity in humankind itself. When he spoke of the superman, he didn't mean a genetically superior race in the same way the Nazis interpreted it, but rather that humankind would now evolve into super God-like beings – all of us, not just a chosen few. Instead of this existential approach denying God, it makes a god of our existence itself.

Dostoevsky, by putting words into the mouths of his characters in *Crime and Punishment* and other writings also announced his belief that the God he was brought up to believe in was dead, and that in his place was one's own conscience or consciousness. In doing so, he implied our need for a subjective rather than objective approach to life, as well as that our lives are the product of our own consciousness. In making consciousness the progenitor, he laid the groundwork for Freud.

Freud denied the existence of an outside God by making God out of consciousness itself. By demonstrating the power inherent in our conscious, unconscious, and subconscious minds, he gave birth to psychotherapy and laid the foundation for the mental sciences. Freud laid the groundwork for us to realize that we are consciousness with physical bodies rather than bodies with consciousness, and to ultimately recognize that that consciousness is God.

In saying that "God is dead," these three men introduced something that was far more important than a new definition of divinity. By exalting the power inherent in consciousness rather than our continuing to conceive of God as a super, all-powerful, punishing, and rewarding demigod, they were saying that a subjective approach to life accomplishes what we have previously attributed to divinity. They were hinting that a change was evolving that would make invisibles more powerful than visibles. It took a while for their viewpoint to affect theology, but by mid-century God-consciousness, defined by theologian Paul Tillich as "the ground of being," was widely accepted, and the possibility of accepting the belief of personal divinity became more than fantasy.

2. The Atom-Splitting Implication

*T*he most important, consciousness-affecting occurrence of the twentieth century happened when we split the atom. When the full implications of what took place almost sixty years ago are understood, we will see how it seeded our current world conflicts. When the spiritual significance of the shift in consciousness introduced by this scientific event is recognized, we will understand why it deserves such a prominent place in our spiritual evolution. The splitting of the atom signaled the end of the dominance of materiality or the objective approach. It announced the primacy of consciousness – subjective motivation. The splitting of the atom means that nothing of a material nature is guaranteed survival.

Ever since the beginning of civilization, every culture has believed that there is some kind of spiritual basis for life.

Along with that belief came rules of conduct that were supposed to make spirituality applicable to daily life. However, in actuality, the first law of human nature, material survival, usually took precedence over subjective idealism. Putting bread on the table superseded altruistic goals as the *modus operandi* of existence. What could be seen, touched, tasted, or smelled came first, but when we split the atom, which is the substance of everything that exists at the material level, we ended the dominance of the material or objective approach to life. We didn't split the atom by finding a greater material power but by the subjective power of consciousness.

Actually, the priority of putting spiritual principle or consciousness first was in the teachings of mystics such as Jesus and Gautama the Buddha. However, in mass acceptance that belief didn't begin to move from speculation to empirical fact until the atom was split. The most important result of splitting the atom is not the creation of a super power base or the discovery that the energy stored in a single atom can transform our daily lives. Its primary importance is that it pinpoints our need for a major shift in priorities.

Man has always recognized the need for both a spiritual and material approach to life, but until the splitting of the atom took his top priority had been to achieve material goals, and any spiritual or altruistic solution for the fulfillment of his needs was secondary. But when the atom was split by the spirit or consciousness within human beings, the realization that consciousness is more important to us than effects moved from speculation to logic. Despite the fact that mystics taught that "in the beginning was the Word… and the Word was made flesh," until now objective concerns have taken precedence over spiritual principle. Cause precedes effects. "In the beginning" is an idea that comes from subjective thinking, after which that idea manifests in form. If I want to bake a cake, I first get the idea, the recipe or word, and then I acquire flour, eggs, sugar, etc., and a couple of hours later I have a cake. The cake, in turn, reflects the quality of the word, or precept, I have chosen.

The problem that current societies now face is that most of our institutions, including governments, are based primarily on the old priority of perpetuating material conditions. Materialistic goals continue to take precedence over spiritual or altruistic values. In America we claim that "In God we trust," but in actuality, if we do not get what we want expediently through diplomacy, we send in the military and allow materialistic objectives to take precedence over subjective idealism.

It seems obvious that if we were to spend as much money on subjective values like education, consensus management, and the feeding, clothing, and housing of the world's poor, as we do on weapons of mass destruction, we wouldn't have any need to protect ourselves against terrorists because there wouldn't be any. Most of the world's chaos, whether in our personal lives, our national priorities, our religious institutions, or our industries happens because putting objective results as our top priority no longer works, and the new subjective or spiritual approach has not yet been incorporated. When the spiritual effect of the splitting the atom is completely understood, we will solve our crisis of perception, and subjective values will become primary.

3. The Importance of One

*I*f Uncle Gilbert had lived to the end of the twentieth century, he would have seen his advice to keep it simple express itself in a most extraordinary way – a shift in consciousness to an awareness of the importance of One. Nothing is simpler than One; complications begin when we try to encompass the many. A change in priority is emerging that seems to go against collective socialization. If properly instituted, the growing awareness of the importance of each individual actually shows us how we can successfully live together.

Making One preeminent represents a complete reversal of the direction society has taken for thousands of years. Even in our earliest civilizations, the direction has always been toward more, bigger, and more powerful. Families became clans, clans became states, and states became nations. As civilizations progressed, larger nations dominated weaker nations, always more, bigger, and stronger, until now the United States has emerged as the preeminent world power; however, now there is a tendency heading toward the importance of and even the dominance of the small – of *One.*

When one young man on a tiny island in the Philippines can get on his computer, shut down whole nations, and cost the world's businesses billions of dollars by putting the words "I love you" on the Internet, that signifies the power inherent in one seemingly insignificant person. When one terrorist can put a single bomb on a plane and cause us to spend a billion dollars every day examining luggage at all the world's airports, that is telling us that individual terrorists are more effective than whole armies.

Today, our supposedly all-powerful, developed countries no longer have major problems with each other, but face a dilemma and threat to their financial and ecological survival over what to do about the small third-world countries. As of now, industry downsizing is in style and giant companies, such as A.T.& T., find it better to break up into smaller companies. That shows that valuing small over bigger is in our financial consciousness as well. On top of that, globalization is running rampant and affecting each one of us politically, economically, and socially, without any powerful nation or group directing or controlling it.

Finally, when the world's most powerful country has an election that hung on single votes, that tells us something – that each individual who votes is important. If nothing more, it showed that we can no longer say, "My one vote won't make a difference." In fact, it revealed that the very essence of democracy rests on the importance of each individual.

The only way to experience who we really are is for us to stop being in awe of the big and start seeing the wonder of the small. Under the guise of being offered spiritual enlightenment, we have been taught to transcend the finite rather than to love it. Institutions that denigrate individualism by encouraging conformity subordinate the single for the whole and deny the sacredness of the small.

Everything starts and ends with One. When socialization caused the well-being of the individual to be inferior to the aims of organizations, churches, and nations, wars became inevitable. I believe that when concern for the individual takes precedence over national interests, war itself will cease to exist. Surprisingly, a couple of years ago, our United States military establishment came out with a new slogan, "The Army of One." I wonder if they understood the New Age meaning of what they were proclaiming.

I have just touched on three examples of the birth and maturing of consciousness that has taken place during the twentieth century: the death of an objective concept of God, the spiritual implication of splitting the atom, and the importance of One. Each of these examples was meant to illustrate how consciousness is taking us to new levels of awareness in preparation for our individually experiencing the spiritual condensate.

Chapter 3

The Mind Instrument

*B*efore I attempt to explain what it means to experience the dimension I call the Third Appearance, I feel I must add to the groundwork I have been laying by addressing the connection between consciousness and the mind, the limits of the thinking mind, and the resulting superstitions it gives birth to. Having discerned that there is a difference between consciousness and the mind, science has long been dissecting the human brain in order to figure out how the mind works.

So far, it has been unsuccessful. Theirs is an objective or physiological approach dealing with the constitution and mechanics of the brain rather than with how it is used. I am sure that once scientists discover how our minds operate, we will be better able to keep from misusing them.

Until now I've been talking subjectively about the perceptions we entertain without including the object with which we produce them. The mind is our mental instrument, a tool used in aid of our perceptions. Once we learn how to use it objectively, we will no longer be in danger of being used by it. Scientists will continue to be baffled by the workings of the mind until they understand how it relates to consciousness.

Over a hundred years ago the metaphysical movement came about because people discovered that the thinking mind played an important part in translating spiritual ideals and goals into practical application. They found that by thinking we human beings become conversion machines, converting idea into form through the use of mental energy.

In order to close the gap between the divine and the human and to make us aware of our individual responsibility, we have to realize that we have a co-creator relationship between our thinking minds and the creative principle of life. Basically that is true, but if we each as individuals also represent the presence of that creative energy, what then does co-creatorship mean? What is the relationship between spirit and the thinking process?

When the metaphysical movement was first established, they spelled the word "mind" with a capital M, and it was often substituted for the word "God." Though metaphysics is still referred to as "mind science" or "science of mind," it is more accurate to say that, like psychology, metaphysics is the science of how to use the mind, or mind over matter.

When the early metaphysicians found that through positive thinking, and what they called mental "treatment" they could change conditions, many fell into the trap of making a God out of the mind itself. In the process they dehumanized themselves. Fortunately, the intellect is no longer considered to be endowed with divine power in the way that it was in the past. Rather, the mind is considered to be more a depository of facts than a decision maker. How we subjectively perceive and intuit those facts is what makes things happen.

We ordinarily think of the mind objectively as a thinking instrument, even though its real purpose is subjective. The mind should be understood to be a seeing instrument, an instrument of vision that we use to turn perception or intuition into knowing. As a mental instrument it interprets the conditions that spirit or consciousness creates. The conscious or subconscious activity of the mind is what translates our perceptions into material reality.

As such, the mind is not a power – it's a tool. We need it in the same way Michelangelo needed a chisel. He couldn't scratch the Pieta out of a piece of dense marble with his fingernails, but to believe that his thinking mind was the power rather than his subjective consciousness is a false belief that confuses the power of perception with thought.

Thinking is quantitative – it defines the shape and size of what it reflects upon. Perception is qualitative, which is to say that the situations resulting from our perceptions reflect the values inherent in our consciousness. One can imitate or reproduce with the mind alone, but original creativity is an action of spirit or consciousness. Perceptions precede invention. Through intuition an artist or inventor perceives a possibility and then his or her mind becomes the tool used to project perception into form. The mind does not create, and when the thinking mind preempts intuition, logic is substituted for mysticism. First comes vision, consciousness, intuition, or spirit, and together those then utilize the mind in order to turn perception into material reality.

When my first book, *The Double Thread*, was published in 1967, my publishers referred to me as a "modern mystic." My sister, a Methodist minister's wife, had a fit. She thought of mystics as half-naked, bedraggled men sitting cross-legged contemplating their navels. The dictionary says that mysticism is the belief that one can turn to his or her own inner source of intuition or knowledge for answers. Today, because of the glut of information coming at us from so many directions, it is impossible for any of us to gather all the facts that exist before making decisions; so we must all be mystics. We may accumulate enough facts to inspire our intuition, but then we must listen in order to decide what to do. Techniques of meditation are no more or less than a way to gain control of the thinking mind, clean out the rubbish, and let our individual divine intuition take over.

~   At last the time has come when we can free ourselves from being physically and mentally manipulated by our minds. We can listen to and follow our intuition, or spirit. With our evolved understanding we can now perceive ourselves as the moving force that uses our minds and bodies as the instruments that make it possible for us to create the world we want.

The psychic, Edgar Cayce, was often quoted as saying "Mind is the builder," but in fact that is only a half-truth. He actually said, "Mind is the builder, the spirit is the life," meaning that the mind is the tool of the spirit, and the quality of our perceptions is the active creative energy that uses the mind.

Our co-creator relationship is not an objective affair between a creative source we commonly call God and ourselves. It is the subjective relationship between our minds and our spirit. We need both. We need our minds in order to translate our intuition into action so that at the objective level we know how to proceed. Our inner vision will project itself through our minds to set the wheels in motion. Our mental contemplations open the door to the spirit. If the intellect does not co-create with the spirit, our meditation is sterile, and if the mind is not used as a tool for interpreting the experience, it, too, is wasted.

~   We are never dealing with anything that is outside our own consciousness. There is a necessity for having a co-creative relationship between our intellect and our spirit, but in that co-creator relationship we have a priority – to seek first guidance from spirit, the subjective nature of life. A house divided is one in which the spirit and the mind are at odds with each other.

In the past I knew something was wrong when I was told that I had to renounce my material sense of self, or that to "die daily" meant that I was to deny Walter, my human self. My objective human self, like Michelangelo's chisel, is needed. I need Walter. But I must double-think and be aware that there is a higher, invisible, divine self included in my being that is Walter's power and control.

Double-Thinking

The spiritual condensate level of consciousness is incomprehensible without the ability to double-think. When self-discovery, or self-fulfillment, became a conscious occupation in the twentieth century, like countless others I began to search for psychological and/or spiritual truths that would explain who I was. Though I was rabidly studying the world's religions and psychological treaties while searching for the truth, I wasn't successful because I hadn't yet realized that there are no truths. That is to say, there are no truths that stand alone. I came across truths that I believed were true, and when they didn't work I became frustrated but thought something was wrong with me. What I didn't realize was that at the less-than-absolute level of this world a single truth alone, without some additional truth to complement it, although true, becomes a half-truth.

As human beings we live at the so-called third dimensional level of time and space – the level of multiplicity where everything needs something additional to fulfill it. For instance, knowledge is paramount, but knowledge that is not complemented by experience is meaningless. Experience that is not backed up with knowledge of what has been experienced is useless. In the same manner, love that is not complemented by loving action is fraudulent, and action that is not based on love is fruitless. Most of us who have achieved our desired goals have done so because, consciously or subconsciously, we have combined half-truths into whole ones by employing what I call "double-thinking," a phrase I borrowed from ~~Alwell~~'s *1984* and Aldus Huxley's *Brave New World*.   Orwell's

— I didn't come up with my concept of the need for us to consciously double-think as an intellectual gimmick. In my attempt to close the gap between my human and my divine selves, I felt like a man with one foot on the dock and the other on a boat that was drifting away. I desperately needed to find a way to reconcile my subjective and objective natures in order to cope. My solution was to consciously and consistently double-think, to be aware of material appearances, and simultaneously be aware of what they symbolized. There is no way we, as humans, can truly accept ourselves as the presence of divinity without the ability to double-think.

As simplistic as it may sound, double-thinking is the ability to consciously and consistently entertain two or more aspects of a situation simultaneously without confusing them and thus denying individuality. It is the ability to stand aside and look at a situation from two or more viewpoints at the same time, without losing sight of any of them. It is then that the whole, multi-dimensional truth can be arrived at pragmatically.

Double-thinking is one of those inclusive ways of thinking that the young take for granted. I was talking to a group of teenagers recently and mentioned that when I was young my mother wouldn't let me listen to the radio until I had finished my homework. One of the girls popped up and said, "When I have the stereo on and the TV, it frees up part of my mind so that I can study." That concept is hard for my generation to digest, but it is true.

I wrote *The Double Thread* to emphasize the importance of our being able to see that nothing in life is either-or, especially our divinity and our humanity. Each aspect of ourselves alone is a half-truth of who we are. Together they constitute our wholeness. It takes double-thinking to make half-truths into whole ones. Nevertheless, this double-thread concept was not openly and enthusiastically received until recently.

I have introduced the subject of double-thinking at this time because as we go deeper and deeper into an understanding of the spiritual condensate, the conclusions that I draw will not make sense unless my readers will be able to hold one view point in a state of suspension until its sometimes seemingly contradictory complements are added.

On the one hand, we have to be aware of and listen to the subjective, impersonal, or invisible level of life. On the other hand, we have to double-think and be consciously aware of and concerned about the existence of our parallel visible objective, personal, neighbor level. When we double-think, those two dimensions of our being fall into place without confusing what each is saying, and instead of half-truths we enjoy whole ones.

Roadblocks

𝒰p until this point I have been attempting to clarify and recondition some of our old ways of thinking. In order to move forward it is time for me to expose some of our inherited superstitions. Though we now find fraudulent some of the sacred-cow concepts we have habitually accepted, many of those beliefs were right for us at certain stages of our individual spiritual evolution. I had to believe them myself before I could graduate to the next, more honest level of spiritual understanding. Science has laid the groundwork that makes it possible to expose some reasonable sounding half-truths that have led many well-intended spiritual seekers into unintentional contradictions that have blocked their progress.

   –   As I began to make a list of the superstitions I felt deserved clarification, Uncle Gilbert's commission to "keep it simple" strangled my thought process. I couldn't go on because I couldn't continue without using some language that I felt might automatically trigger old prejudices and understandably repel many in today's world who are put off by traditional religious jargon. If I were to spend pages redefining those words, simplicity would go out the window. On the other hand, I have spent a lifetime reinterpreting some commonly used religious words in the hope that they can become free of old superstitious conditioning and become bridges from the past into a new understanding of spirituality.

Many of us, with good reason, get hot under the collar when someone quotes Scripture in a feeble attempt to authenticate his or her beliefs, and many people cringe when they hear others claim that the Bible is the word of God – as though it wasn't compiled by human beings. There are also those who are annoyed when people refer to the Judeo-Christian tradition as the final word, or who stop listening when people employ religious language in order to appear profound. This is all quite understandable, and I feel the same way.

Our cultural and religious myths are not fantasies. The truths found in any age become the myths of the following age. Even the Greek myths were based on actual happenings. In the retelling, as the years pass, myths can become distorted and require a reinterpretation that fits the present. Our challenge is to discover the truths existing in the old myths that apply to today. We can do that by shifting our attention away from a purely objective story line interpretation into a deeper awareness of the myth's underlying subjective meaning.

—   In writing this book I intended to avoid references to the Scriptures of our Western world Judeo-Christian myth, and I sought to avoid using traditional words that have overt religious connotations. I wanted to explain things in everyday, factual terms that would appeal to everyone, even those readers who have an aversion to words and phrases that smack of theological implication. But I find that there is a reason I am unable to do so.

Despite the fact that the most blatant injustices and inequities have been perpetuated by the way religious sects of all faiths have interpreted their myths for devious purposes, we as individuals are never free until we come to terms with the cultural myths of our heritage. That doesn't mean we have to accept them in the way they have been handed down to us. Because we were raised in a particular society, many disturbing concepts and false judgments have been planted in our unconscious mind of which we are not even aware. If we can look at our myths in a new way, freed of traditional interpretation, some of those old unconscious blockages can be flushed out.

The plays of Shakespeare are alive today because seminal truths are embedded in them – while the plays of many lesser playwrights are forgotten. In the same way, the Judeo-Christian myth has stayed alive for so many years because there is a profound energy in some of the underlying truths that are tucked away in it.

—   It doesn't make any difference whether or not Jesus actually existed, whether he said or did not say the things attributed to him, or whether or not his story is accurate. When they are freed of religious distortion, either the truths embodied in the teachings attributed to Jesus work, or they don't. It all depends on how they are interpreted and applied; that's what is important.

I don't believe that we have to accept the Judeo-Christian story in the way it has been taught; however, some valuable underlying principles may have gotten through to us despite the distortions that are the result of the theological process. I don't want to leave old false concepts festering in our unconscious minds as long as we can reinterpret them in a meaningful way.

Exploring oriental and other religious myths can add other valuable perspectives that can help clarify and make us aware of hidden meanings that exist in our own myth. However, we in the West will never be completely free until we come to terms with the primary myth that has conditioned the society in which we live.

Personally, I owe a debt of gratitude for my visits to the Vedanta monastery in the late 40s and early 50s where a master, Swami Prabvananda, opened my eyes in a way that made it possible for me to appreciate my Judeo-Christian heritage in a different light.

There's a reason that the Bible, our social textbook, has lost the dominant position it has had until recent times. To a great extent our universal media explosion, the ever-expanding internet, and the plethora of print material that reaches our bookshelves daily, constantly compete for our attention and have preempted the Bible's importance for many – particularly the young. Up until the last century when radio, TV, and the movies became popular, the Bible was our cable television. It was our leading source of soap opera scandals and human interest stories – a gold mine of social and spiritual exploration wrapped up in one transportable entertainment package.

I was brought up in a traditional early twentieth century home where the Bible was fed to us on a regular basis, like doses of cod liver oil. As a result I had no appetite for it, until something unexpected happened to me in Hawaii at age thirty. I was visiting a teacher who took me over to the island of Maui to attend a lecture he was giving. While my friend was having appointments, I borrowed a car and went up to the rim of Halealaka, the world's largest extinct volcanic crater. No one told me that short pants and a T-shirt wouldn't do at ten-thousand-eight-hundred feet; so to get out of the chilling wind I got off the path and found a cave-like shelter. I sat there meditating, waiting for the mists to clear so that I could see into the crater, and I experienced something similar to hearing a tape recording in my head. It was on the subject of love. Out of that meditation came the most important revelation of my life; I saw what I now consider to be the secret and central message of the teaching we associate with the man, Jesus.

He said that the only way we can fulfill the laws set forth in the Ten Commandments is for us to dispense with all but one of them and thus get rid of the paranoid "thou shall not" laws. He added that to the remaining First Commandment we should add another, and that if we can reconcile these two commandments we will have the answer to a perfect life – a life that will fulfill all the aims intended by following the Ten Commandments. He gave us two commandments – an apparent duality – as the only way to arrive at a true unity, or non-duality.

Jesus said to love God, which in modern language means to love cause, the invisible creative source of life – and then he said for us to love our neighbors as ourselves, to love effects, which are the visible results of that which caused them to come into being. He also added that if we could love both cause and effect equally we would find that they are the same. He hinted that if we could do that we would close the gap between our divine and human selves and arrive at the condensate level where cause and effect, or the objective and the subjective, are one and the same.

⌐   I took Jesus' two commandments to mean that I am not to think of myself as either a man of earth or a man of God. I'm *both*, and though they are different dimensions of the One that I am, my job in life is to get my two selves to communicate with each other so that eventually they will act as one. The playwright John van Druten, in his introduction to Joel Goldsmith's *The Infinite Way*, addressed our either-or dilemma and the need to double-think in an eloquent way. He said,

> *Always the answers, as they have been revealed have remained somehow apart, 'out there', set off from man in his daily life and the facts of his daily living, so that there has grown up a kind of unfortunate snobbery on the subject, as though it were somehow vulgar to expect tangible or practical results, and man has been forced into a fatal dualism, trying to live on two planes at once, the material and the spiritual, both apparently equally real, yet without any understandable relation to each other, like a firm composed of two partners who are not on speaking terms.*

The two partners are the two commandments; one represents our need to perceive ourselves and our lives subjectively, based on inner or spiritual values, and the other partner is the one who sees himself objectively and bases his life on achieving visible results. One is arrived at by intuition and one is conceptualized by logic. It's not either-or. The success of the partnership depends on both partners' equal responsibility to communicate.

⌐   Real understanding is always both subjective and objective. If we see a drunk in the gutter, we know subjectively what got him there. He didn't love himself so he turned to an object, a bottle of whisky, to give him what he thought he lacked. On the other hand, we can go to a fancy cocktail party and see a healthy and successful looking man wearing a $2,000 Armani suit and compulsively slugging down his martinis as though his life depended on them. From this objective observation we know that if he doesn't change his consciousness, he will end up in his own personal gutter.

The same principle applies at the level of our local and national governments, our institutions, and the individuals we work with. If governments advocate objective approaches, such as dropping bombs or putting financial pressure on other nations to get what they want, sooner or later they will end up victims of their own techniques. When institutions are more interested in the bottom line than in offering a service, they will eventually end up in the bankruptcy court. However, when nations or individuals are motivated primarily by altruistic, subjective values, such as eliminating the need to drop bombs, caring more about the cause of poverty than its effect, and caring more about individual rights than supporting dictators, heaven and earth will be one and the same.

⸺ The two commandments to love God and our neighbor tell us that nothing is either-or. Sounds simple, doesn't it? Nevertheless, either-or thinking is, and always has been, the major cause of conflict, the mother of exclusivity, and the very thing that has kept us in material and spiritual bondage. Think about it and you will see that an either-or attitude still dominates politics and preempts open discussions of value. Inevitably, heated discussions dissolve into a split with one conclusion taking precedence over the other. It is either-or thinking that breeds superstition.

The Superstition of Faith

*I*n order to make the spiritual condensate understandable I have to now enter a sensitive area by exposing some of the major superstitions that science is helping to dispel. *Webster's Unabridged Dictionary* defines superstition as "any belief or attitude that is inconsistent with the known laws of science." It also interprets superstition as being "any belief or attitude that is inconsistent with what is considered to be true and rational."

The rationale for most of the world's wars has been based on a superstitious belief in God, with each side believing that their faith in God will win the war for them. The underlying reason for going to war might have been material gain, but the excuse for doing it was most often attributed to God's will. As long as wars and acts of terrorism are excused in the name of God, superstition rules.

We can't sober up to reality and get rid of our religious hangovers until we stop believing that endorsing superstition is a prerequisite for spirituality. It's surprising how many of our traditional beliefs, relevant to how our good is to come about and how our desires are to be fulfilled, is founded on superstition. In this respect I'm sorry that we are not like computers with delete buttons that we can push and instantly send old superstitions into the trash bin.

— All too often, protestations of faith are no more than endorsed superstition. No matter how often we have been told that we should have faith – as though faith is a faucet that can be turned on and off – it has most often been based on the superstitious belief that appealing to a power or supreme being apart from our own higher consciousness can give us what we want or need. The belief that there is anything affecting our lives that is not related to our own consciousness is superstition. At last, thanks to our scientists, we are now able to replace such superstitions with fact based on data which proves that through our perceptions, we can literally affect matter.

Saying that religious faith can now be replaced by fact sounds cold and heretical, doesn't it? It isn't. We should shout with joy and dance in the streets because realizations that have evolved through scientific empiricism now take the guesswork out of faith. Blind faith can now be replaced by eye-opening knowledge.

Traditionally, having faith has always been centered on there being some object to have faith in – a God of some sort. There had to be some object that one had faith in – be that a person, a teaching, a church, or a supreme being. Now we know that there is no mysterious code or spiritual lottery that will magically fulfill our desires. Our good comes from the infinity of our own consciousness and we recognize that it is superstition to believe there is anything to call upon outside of that which our own consciousness can supply.

There are no accidents in consciousness; cause and effect are one. To believe that by an act of faith we can make something happen that is not already happening is like having faith that at some future time two-times-two will be four. Knowing tells us that two-times-two is now and always has been four. Experiencing the truth of mathematics frees us from superstition, but having faith that two-times-two is four is a waste of time and won't change the answer one way or the other.

When I say that fact replaces faith, it is because our growing capacity to know that our perceptions create our reality eliminates the need for superstition-based explanations of paranormal events and unexplainable seemingly miraculous healings. Now there is nothing in the way of our knowing the unknown apart from the limitations we place on ourselves. We now know the reason that right thinking or right perceptions are causal, and, being free of superstition, we can be personally in control of our lives. Yes, we have faith – faith in our ability to know true cause and how and why the spiritual process affects us.

— We may not always know why specific actions produce right results, but we can remove ourselves from believing in superstitious causes by knowing that we alone are the instigators of the results we wish to attain. It isn't as though we have faith in right thinking or right perceptions; we have faith in our ability to know or find out how and why they operate so that we can apply them correctly and free ourselves from superstition. There is no accident or chance about it. Masters in any field do not say, "I believe;" they know.

In order for our beliefs to become fruitful, they must reach a certain experiential reality before they can turn into knowing. Just as water has to reach a certain temperature before it boils, beliefs have to be experienced in consciousness in order for them to become living realities and transcend superstition. When that happens, knowing becomes a kind of spiritual energy that turns into a self-fulfilling prophecy rather than fantasy.

No one can fulfill another's expectations; it is up to the individual. Yet each of us, through an act of free will, can become alive as our expectations become consciously activated through realization, through knowing. When that happens we experience a higher dimension of our being freed of limitations – then we will know what Paul meant when he said, "YE ARE GODS."

The Cause and Effect Superstition

*T*here is no more potent superstition than the belief that effects are cause. When the so-called metaphysical movement began to make an impact on America at the beginning of the twentieth century, and Christian Science churches began to appear, quantum physicists had not yet proposed their concept that consciousness was the creative, maintaining, and sustaining cause of material effects. Nevertheless, the success of Christian Science at that time was based on the teaching that there is no cause in effects, that Spirit or Divine Principle is the only cause.

If it were generally accepted, the belief that effects are not cause would put Madison Avenue advertising agencies out of business. Every TV commercial sets out to convince the public that its product can cause something desirable to happen. It's the same with the pharmaceutical suppliers who try to convince the public that its health depends on an advertised drug. Until superstition is replaced by a true understanding of the relationship of cause and effect, the power of consciousness will continue to play second fiddle to the belief that effects are cause.

If the quantum physicists are correct, no one has ever been killed by a bullet. We can put a bullet on a table and wait for it to kill someone, but we will have a long wait. There is no intelligence in a bullet. Someone had to consciously make the bullet, someone else had to consciously put it in a gun, consciously aim the gun, and consciously pull the trigger. The consciousness of those who manufactured the guns and bullets and of the one who pulled the trigger killed the person, not the bullet itself. An atomic bomb cannot drop itself, nor can an act of terrorism come about of itself. It takes the consciousness of men to make these things happen. Consciousness, not effects, is cause, and it is a form of superstition to believe otherwise. Knowing that consciousness or spirit is cause eliminates superstition, and instead of being used by effects one can use them and consequently depend on the power of consciousness as cause.

My understanding of what I just said was a long time coming. My father, grandfather, and uncle were all medical doctors. They were quite vocal about their belief that something should be done about Christian Scientists who, through their misunderstood faith, allowed their children to suffer rather than turning to medical science for help. Those misguided Christian Science parents were correct in having discovered that spirit or consciousness was the ultimate power and that it could produce spontaneous healings, but because they did not double-think, they turned a half-truth into superstition. If they had understood that what medical science had to offer was a by-product of spirit as well, their children might not have suffered.

I finally understood that it's not a matter of whether we use effects or not, but rather of our dependency on them. Spontaneous healings without medical intervention do happen at times, and of course medical science also saves lives. All the wonderful things that science – man's creative ingenuity – and spiritual consciousness produces are here for our use and enjoyment. We can use these effects and not be used by them, if we are aware of and dependent on the consciousness that the effects symbolize rather than on the effects themselves.

I take vitamins, use medications on occasion, and drink a glass of wine when I feel like it, but if I were to find myself being dependent on any of those things I would re-examine my thinking. If I were to be enslaved by the belief that I had to follow a rigid timetable for when, where, or how much to imbibe, it would be a sign of dependence. To be dependent on any created thing is another form of superstition. My dependency is on the consciousness that has created the effects I use, not on the effects themselves.

— Let's look at the ways that, in the name of divinity, we have perpetuated superstition. It is superstitious to believe that good can come to us from some outside source who bestows it upon us. All good already exists. It can only come from us – from our realized consciousness. The belief that the things we need or want are drawn to us by anything other than our own consciousness is superstition.

Fear is superstition at its worst. When a government, church, or organization fosters fear, they enable us in making that superstitious fear into a self-defeating, self-fulfilling prophecy. To believe that there is a supreme being that is in one place and not another, or in one person and not another, is superstition. To believe that others are somehow obligated to take care of our needs, or that our good comes from them personally, is a form of superstition. Your good may come via another person, but if that good is not already in your consciousness it will not become your self-realization. On the other hand, when you appreciate how your spirit enhances your life through or as another person, that is how and why you love that person.

⌐ Our own higher consciousness is life, and life is self-sustained. Consequently, to pray for life to be more alive is superstition. To believe that health, weather, good fortune, companionship, or new opportunities come from something outside of our own consciousness is superstition. All those things can and do come into manifestation by an automatic divine process that is taking place in and as us. They come from our experiencing our own divine higher consciousness. To believe they come from a cause outside of ourselves is superstition at its most delusional.

We become free when we consciously realize that there isn't anything or anyone outside of our own selves that can keep us from self-fulfilling knowledge. Then we become aware of the fact that we can turn on our protective, creative, and rewarding spiritual energy at any time. It not only frees us from the tyranny of undiscovered truths, but it lifts us into the realization that we are now already all that we have thought divinity to be. Even though we appear as finite beings, our potential is limitless.

—   When I say that the answers are all within our own selves, I don't want to take the sense of magic out of life that we may have felt was provided by a supreme being in the past. The fact that the answer to all of our desires is in and as our own consciousness is just as awe-inspiring and amazing as anything can ever be. Our ability to make conscious contact with our own divine consciousness is the "pearl of great price" and the miracle of miracles. When Jesus said, "your faith hath made you whole," he was trying to counter superstition by explaining that he himself, apart from representing the potential in all of us, hadn't done anything miraculous. The person's own perception and consciousness, or faith, had done it. Jesus was the first person who voiced the truth that one's own conscious realization becomes that person's self-fulfilling prophecy. In other words we don't have to look outside of our ownselves for our good.

Jesus also said, "Whatever ye shall ask in prayer, believing ye shall receive...all things." He was saying that if a person's belief reaches the experiential level where the energy of knowing comes into being, it becomes a self-fulfilling prophecy for that person. That which one perceives automatically comes about. "I hope," "I believe," and "I have faith" all endorse superstition, but

"I know" says "It is," and whatever is envisioned experientially becomes fact.

The God Word

I have hesitated before using the word, "God," up until now, because, though every language includes a word that stands for the recognition of some kind of divine presence or principle of ultimate value, in many instances the word "God" has been used as an excuse for man's most devastating cruelties. It has been used as a psychological tool to subdue and control people, to cause them to hate other sects that have different concepts of God, and it has been the politician's excuse for perpetrating most all of the world's wars. Even today, people kill each other to defend their concepts of God. The most widely accepted beliefs in God are based on superstition, and man's devious nature has taken advantage of it to accomplish his own selfish and bigoted ends.

In order to cease using God as a justification for our ill-conceived actions, there is one thing we must do. We must stop believing in God as something other than and apart from ourselves. Believing in God in the traditional religious way constitutes a denial of personal responsibility. Such belief may help lead to an experience of God consciousness, but unless God consciousness is actually experienced, and ultimately experienced as one's own consciousness, believing in God becomes a superstitious stumbling block.

In the early 1970s I visited my friend, Lama Govinda, at his ashram on the border of Tibet. During one of our conversations, I used the word "God." He stopped me and said, "Find another word. God comes from the Old Testament where God was thought of as a father figure." Govinda thought that I was referring to the traditionally objective concept of God. I told him that I didn't think of God that way, and that for me to use another word would just leave the old one rotting in my unconscious. I use the word "God" as a one-word metaphor for the life process, as shorthand for creation, and I hope that those of you who have trouble with the word will forget its ordinary implication when you come across it in this manuscript. Translate God into your own best concept of a universal principle of life and behavior, or as an underlying reality that is the reason of all life and creativity. There is no way we can close the gap between our divinity and our humanity as long as we are unable to perceive some ultimate cause or creative source of life free of superstition, whether we call it God, the divine process, or have some other way of identifying it.

Meister Eckhart, the thirteenth-century mystic, said that if God did not exist, man would have had to create him. There are two sides to that statement. First, it isn't that our concept of God in itself does anything, but without a concept for us to experience, the energy of creation would not be activated. Even though there isn't any recognized God apart from our own experienced consciousness, believing in God-consciousness can lead to an experience that does the things we have previously attributed to God. When Jesus said, "Your faith hath made you whole," he was saying that it was the person's own personally experienced consciousness that made him or her whole. The experience of God-consciousness is God – not a superstitious belief in God.

Secondly, the other reason we create concepts of a God apart from our own consciousness is to let ourselves off the hook. As long as we think there is a God out there to believe in, our belief in God is the excuse we give ourselves for not being the presence of God.

We may become spiritually sophisticated and say that

we believe in the existence of a Christ or God-consciousness, but that, too, turns God into a concept – a noun – and becomes our attempt to avoid the responsibility for actively living out of our own higher God-consciousness. We have no choice in the matter any more; *we must now start being the presence of God – just believing in it is not enough.*

What I am proposing is the most difficult proposition mankind has ever faced. As human beings we were born with finite size and limitations; therefore, as long as we think of ourselves as bodies it seems incongruous to assume that we are the presence of an unlimited infinite divine presence. It is much easier for us to believe that there is a God outside of ourselves.

We in the West tend to predominantly objectify our beliefs and picture them in some kind of form. We portray God as a powerful old man, and we carve and paint statues representing Jesus, Mary, Joseph, and others. When we pray to them we believe that we are praying to the people represented by those pictures and statues rather than the consciousness they symbolize. We are horrified when we visit temples in India and see people bowing before grotesque figures with hideous animal faces or multiple arms. Because we objectify our beliefs we do not understand that people of other cultures may be praying subjectively to the ideas that their statues symbolize, rather than believing that those images have actually existed in some place or time.

If we need something objective to identify with, there is something we can do. We can personalize God as the presence of our own higher or divine consciousness. We can think of our own divine consciousness as a physical presence within and converse with it in the way many feel they are doing when they pray to a God outside of themselves.

Our past successes have taken place without our actually

knowing why. At those times when we accomplished our desired goals by superstitiously calling on God, we were successful not because of an outside influence but rather because we had actually experienced our own God-selves. Contacting our higher divine consciousness is what produced the results we wanted even though we didn't realize it. No matter how or when truth is experienced, it effectively transforms conditions.

The key to attaining a God experience without surrendering personal responsibility, without believing in a God outside ourselves, is possible when we intentionally double-think and we are consciously aware that we have two or more levels of self operating at the same time. It is possible for us to be aware of our limited personal-sense selves while at the same time being aware of the existence of our higher consciousness – the I AM God experience. It not only can be done, but it must be done if we are to add to the critical mass of those who have already experienced God-consciousness. It is that collective consciousness which is destined to set a course that will save the world from self-destruction.

Just as there are no two of us alike, there are no two concepts of God that are the same. When we contemplate a Supreme Presence, or God, our concept is made up of the values we cherish and include within our spiritual repertoires. A domineering and controlling person sees God as a domineering and controlling force, while a gentle and loving soul sees God as a benevolent and loving presence. It isn't that man is made in the image of God; it is that we concocted our concepts of God in the image of ourselves, and of the supreme values we entertain in our own consciousness.

There are God concepts that are no more than opiates for dulling the reasoning capacities of those who allow themselves to be controlled by institutions. However, in this increasingly tumultuous time, man's survival depends on his identifying with and actually being consciously in tune with the creative source of his life. To resist using the traditional word for that source can end up being a kind of atheistic materialism, and those who do so won't be free until they either come to terms with their old concept of God or reinvent a new meaning for it.

Reinventing God

*I*n reinventing a meaning for God it is easier to state what God isn't than what God is. God isn't something or someone you can ask for favors. Like the sun, the spirit isn't aware of whom it shines upon, saint or sinner. God is not doing anything at one moment that it is not doing at another, and God is not doing something for one person that it is not doing for another. God is not in one place and not another.

To free ourselves from a superstitious belief in God we have to consciously impersonalize it. That means we have to see God as a universal higher consciousness or intelligence that exists everywhere – including within each of us. This impersonal God won't give us something tomorrow that it is not giving us today. If there were a God that would withhold our good, we would have to hate that God. If God were powerful enough to destroy evil and wasn't doing it, that God would be a monster. Wanting something from God implies that God chooses when to give and when not to. Attributing good or evil to God supports the belief that God is a personality. God is not a "he" that either rewards or punishes. *God is Spirit or higher consciousness and nothing else.*

It is almost impossible to impersonalize our own higher consciousness because the minute we think of it as being ours, we have personalized it. Divine consciousness is the same in all living beings. The only difference is in the veils of ignorance that separate understanding from reality. Every person in the world has access to divine consciousness though very few see through the veil. Very few have moved from an objective concept of God into subjective reality.

Mystics of the past intuited that our mental veils have hidden the truth from us, and they have tried to explain it by saying that "Maya," "this world," or "personal sense" was an illusion that we had to get rid of. The problem is that they didn't take their conclusion far enough. By saying that personal sense is illusion, they simply substituted one veil for another. The illusion is the denial of the presence of higher consciousness in each person, rather than revealing it as an available personal experience.

Once more, the key to our attaining a God experience without surrendering personal responsibility (by believing in a God outside of ourselves) is for us to consciously double-think, to consciously be aware that for all practical purposes we have two basic levels of self operating at the same time. It is possible for us to recognize and respond to our personal sense-self and its desire to experience our own higher consciousness, while at the same time also being aware that we are our higher consciousness – *the I AM God experience.*

To believe that once we become aware of God's presence harmony will instantly be produced is also a subtle superstition. Our higher consciousness is the presence of God. God doesn't produce harmony; God is the harmony. God doesn't bring peace; God is peace. God doesn't fulfill us; it is our fulfillment. As long as we believe that we have to do something to make those things happen, we are denying that they are included in our own higher consciousness.

To believe that we have to go to a church or holy place to

find God is superstition. God is a state of consciousness that can be experienced anywhere, not something that can be found in a particular place. Our own higher consciousness is our church or synagogue, and it goes everywhere we go. Whenever we are in God-consciousness we are in church. Whenever we feel the presence of higher consciousness while sharing with others we are in church. There are places where we more easily sense an all-inclusive oneness than in other locations – most often in nature or while listening to inspiring music – and those places are our churches.

Believing that we can change the mind of God by praying, thinking the right thoughts, or believing that we have to tell God about our problems is rank superstition. God doesn't have a mind we can appeal to; God is divine mind. We can't change it, but we can have access to it.

I have compassion for those who still believe in a God that can heal them, because God is not a healer – God is the healing itself. There is a divine healing process that can be realistically accessed through our higher conscious perceptions. Through an experience of a superstitous-free God-consciousness, all things, including healings, that people have previously sought from their superstitious belief in God, come about.

The Shocking Truth

When I am able to tap into my higher consciousness in meditations, sometimes the messages I get from it are shocking to me. New revelations are always shocking because they contradict old beliefs. Some time ago, during one of those morning meditations, I was shaken to hear, "God is not love!" This was quite a shock to me because I had spent years quoting "God is love" from John's epistle.

It's true; God is not love. To believe that God is love is to accept an objective, material interpretation of the word "love." We ordinarily think of love as a noun, a thing, but God is not a thing, not a noun. As Rabbi Cooper says in his book, *God Is A Verb*, "God is an action." Therefore, God is not love; God is lovingness. God is the act of loving, the energy of loving. When you are loving, you are Goding.

The reason that God is not love is because there really aren't any nouns – nouns do not exist. Each noun symbolizes a state of consciousness as it appears in form. Nouns represent the consciousness that has brought whatever is present into being and is that which is maintaining and sustaining it. A table is not a noun; it is an action. We think of it as a table because it functions as a table. You can put a board across a couple of rocks, and if you use it as your table it becomes your table because it acts like a table.

God is not omnipresent. For God to be present, God would have to be an object that is someplace. Subjectively, God is everywhere because God is the activity of omnipresence – but not omnipresent. It is omnipresence. God is "everywhere-ness." God is the action of all-knowingness that we call omniscience. As omnipotence, God is the totality of all energy or power present in every atom.

For someone to call on God, one's higher consciousness, to do something that is not already being done proves that the person thinks of God as a noun. To ask God to do something is like asking the sun to shine. Is there any doubt that despite the clouds that may obscure it, the sun is always shining?

As I said earlier, God doesn't heal anyone; God is the healing process itself. The experience of a healing consciousness affects all the situations and people who come into contact with it. When healing is not being experienced, healing does not exist.

God, your higher consciousness, is a verb. God is not something you believe in, but rather it is the believing itself that is God. The action of believing is the verb that activates perception. When Jesus said, "Your faith hath made you whole," he was saying that your own personal action of faithfulness has made you whole. God is a divine process and when that process is actively at work, God is at work. The only time God consciously exists for you is when it is being lived or experienced by you.

God is not life. God is living or "livingness." The livingness of you is your Godness. You do not exist unless you are being yourself, and you are not consciously being yourself unless you are being God-conscious. When God-consciousness is active, we are aware of being the presence of God. We are not aware of being the presence of God *unless we are consciously experiencing God. When we discover ourselves as active consciousness we will have discovered God.*

The Verb You

*T*he question is not "Who am I?" It's "What am I?" Just as God is not a noun you are not a noun. You are a verb. If you are made in the image of God, and God is a verb, then you are also a verb. Your body may be a noun, but you are that which is actively living your body. You are that which is breathing through your nose, digesting your food, intuiting your actions, and feeling your feelings. To know who you are is to know yourself as the livingness of yourself. You are a verb that is expressing itself as a noun, and your body is that place where your active consciousness becomes visible. The name you go by is your body identification. Your body is your noun, a noun that symbolizes the state of your consciousness. You are not a material statistic. You are consciousness and consciousness is a verb; you are the action that is taking place as the person you appear to be.

Get out your old photo albums and look through them. See who you appeared as at age three, eight, eighteen, forty, and beyond. None of those bodies any longer exists, but you are still here, because you have never been any of them. Instead of being them, you have possessed them. You have always been the active consciousness or livingness that was growing your different bodies. Even now you can mentally stand aside and see your body as your instrument, as the costume you are presently wearing in this stage of your evolution. The way to change that costume is to change the way you perceive it. When your perception changes, your material projection – your noun – changes. That is the secret to what is called a spiritual healing. Illness is a time when we face a crisis of perception. We can't change our perceptions by thinking alone, but as verbs we can experience the change, and when we do the outer picture changes.

If you can think of yourself as a verb, do you still perceive yourself as an individual person? Today the word "individual" has come to mean exactly the opposite of its root meaning. It is thought of as separate from others, solo, or one of a kind. Originally "individual" meant "indivisible" or "one with."

If you are an individual, what are you one with? Obviously, it doesn't mean your physical body. If you were to lose an arm or leg, you wouldn't say "five-sixths of me is here." You would still say "I am here," because you are the verb that is living your body. "I" is your individuality, which is also one with, or indivisible, from the whole. If you see yourself as a noun, there is no way you can agree with the mystics when they say you are made in the image of God.

What are you one with? You are one with universal consciousness or spirit. Your "I" is consciousness or spirit and as such, you are not a part of spirit; you are all that spirit is. You are spirit being itself.

At the personal-sense level, it is nearly impossible to understand how we can be one with or as an infinite allness, and yet be individually unique at the same time, but infinity can't be minus anything, including your unique presence. We can't intellectually comprehend that paradox, but we can feel it. As verbs we can feel it, and when we do we are able to enjoy our individuality and not lose sight of our oneness with all that exists.

When Paul said, "I live, but not I, Christ lives my life," he did not mean that another person was living his life. He was saying that he wasn't a noun, but that his higher consciousness was what was activating his life. When Jesus said, "Destroy this body and in three days I will raise it up," he didn't say, "Destroy this body and in three days I will raise [me] up." Because he knew he was a verb – consciousness – he was not limited to a physical form.

This is another place where double-thinking applies. You are both consciousness and body; you are not either-or. When you are thinking from the objective viewpoint of form rather than cause, you think of yourself as the physical body you see in the mirror. At best, you may understand that your body is a metaphor of your consciousness. Until you are able to get a feeling for what it means to be consciousness with a body, rather than a body with consciousness, it will be difficult for you to accept yourself as the Third Appearance.

If we accept the fact that our consciousness is who we are, then we will know that consciousness is by its very nature active. It, too, is not a thing, not a noun. Then we will experience what Jesus meant when he said, "I AM the way, the truth, and the life." Perhaps he should have said, "I AM [is] the way, the truth, and the life." It's easy to speculate that we are consciousness, but until we can experience ourselves as verbs we are limited by the physical universe.

Try the following experiment. Stop reading for a minute, close your eyes, and feel the livingness of yourself. Sense your aliveness irrespective of your body. Feel yourself as the power within you. See yourself as a verb, as consciousness. That is what you are.

Divine Energy

*I*n this ongoing wrestling match we have between our thinking minds and our spirit, the most difficult thing we must do is to go beyond habitually thinking in terms of good and evil. We are so conditioned to think of the good things as good and the bad as bad that we can't divorce judgment from fact.

We have all heard about unconditional love. It is easy to talk about it, but the minute we try to apply it to something personal, our concept of love becomes conditioned by past judgments. It is impossible for us to keep from judging as long as we primarily analyze results, rather than first centering on cause. In other words, if we want to understand unconditional love we have to see love not only as a verb but also free of either good or bad – using the same formula as our new way of looking at God or the omnipotence we attribute to God.

What I am going to say now is as difficult for me to say as it may be for you to hear. It requires letting go of the lifeline we have held to in all of life's circumstances. It is imperative that we consider this challenging viewpoint if we are to arrive at a self-active and consistent principle of life that will eliminate ignorance and failure and replace them with self-control and success. Because we have habitually attributed the good things in life to love and to God, we have believed love and God are good. They are not!

Love, or God, is neither good nor bad; it is an energy. Indeed, there is a divine purpose in life that is beyond both good and bad, that has no opposite, and is the equivalent of what we think of as good. But if we think of God or of love in terms of good alone, that shows we do not know what it is. Instead, God or love is a kind of energy, and that energy or power can be used in what appears to be either constructive or destructive ways, depending on how we direct it through our perceptions – our spiritual-mental value system.

In his book, *Talks on Truth,* Charles Fillmore, the founder of Unity, equated the energy of love with a magnet. He said that love attracts whatever the "mind" aims it at, good or bad. He goes on to say that the "magnetic energy of love" is impersonal and can equally draw forth lust, greed, or any other human desire when it is aimed at them. It can just as equally evoke beauty, compassion, and unselfish goals when it is focused on them. Through the thoughts we think – the love of money, the love of sex, the love of personal power – we borrow power from love for selfish purposes, and in doing so we can use it to destroy rather than heal.

Christian Science and the metaphysical movement, in general, based their principles of spiritual healing on the belief that since God is the only power there is no power in disease or in a lack of supply, and their belief was rewarded by a considerable number of healings; however, it takes some fancy mental footwork to observe the devastation that follows some diseases and to simultaneously believe that there is no power in them. Where disease is active there is power and energy or it would not exist; however, as God is the only power in either good or bad situations, when disease is present it borrows its power from God consciousness – the only power that exists. Healings take place, not because of one's belief in the non-existence of disease, but because there has been a shift in perception that redirects the energy. If you sufficiently convince yourself that the power in a situation is no longer present you have resolved a crisis of perception and redirected the energy. Your perception that a situation is powerless takes the power away from it.

To believe that love is always used for good is superstition. However, when we release love from labeling it "good" and see it for what it is – the most powerful energy in the universe and the only power capable of transforming the world – we understand its divine purpose and no longer unwittingly direct it toward selfish aims and anti-social results. There are no outside forces, including love, that act on their own; all action is instigated by thought, purpose, and desire. It is up to us to be aware of how we direct that energy, to know how to release it through our faith in its divine purpose, and to understand that through our consciousness we are co-creators with and as that energy. Once we do, love will be directed by our higher consciousness, and it will be the beacon that lights our way.

Scripture tells us that "God is too pure to behold iniquity," and that love shines on the "saint and the sinner." Neither God nor love in its pure unconditioned presence knows anything about good or evil, any more than the wind is cognizant of who it touches. Our problem in understanding God has been that we personalize it as the source of our good, and we are not aware that, like everything else, the presence of that godly energy can be both used and misused.

You may ask, "How can love or God be misused?" Take the energy of electricity, for example. It is most often used for what we think of as good. It lights our homes, provides heat, runs appliances, and yet it can also be used to execute a human being or burn down a house. God and love are the same energy, and when that energy is understood and complemented by knowledge, it can illumine the world.

Man has a faculty through which he receives love. That faculty is his consciousness. Through his consciousness man calls love, the complement of thought, into action. When we indulge in judgments without an understanding of love we may energize hate, discord, and disharmony. When love is expressed selfishly, misguided thought has twisted its purpose. In the same way, when love is directed primarily toward achieving purely material goals, it loses its purity and purpose.

On the opposite end of the spectrum, the subjective substance of a decision dictates its objective manifestation. When the energy of love is directed toward its divine purpose healings, harmony, and joy are the result.

It is of paramount importance to recognize that *love or God is an all-powerful energy, because once we recognize our capacity to use that energy we begin to take responsibility for how we misuse it.* Blind love means just what the words imply. It is the energy of love unaccompanied by wisdom. When we ask daily to be made aware of the energy of love so that we do not inadvertently misdirect it, we will know what it is to peek into heaven.

The Necessity of Evil

Before the spiritual condensate can become more than an intellectual speculation there is one more major gap in our traditional understanding of omnipotence or the divine process of life that must be closed. For centuries theologians have unsuccessfully debated the dilemma of reconciling the presence of evil with an all powerful and infinite God; however, this can't be done unless a purpose for evil is discovered. To accept the idea that there is a purpose for evil is not only an emotionally repugnant concept, but it also discourages us from turning to religion as an escape from reality. Unless we can accept an explanation that justifies the presence of evil in a way that does not insult our intelligence, there is no way we can understand how we can personally see ourselves as divine humans.

I am not saying that evil does not exist or that it is humanly desirable, but rather that it is possible to arrive at a different understanding of how those experiences we define as evil affect our spiritual evolution. I have outlined the impersonal nature of the energy of God, or love, and our need to double-think as necessary conclusions for setting aside the dichotomy of good and evil. Good and evil are opposite sides of a metaphysical coin, and until we understand that concept the coin is worthless.

The paradox is that once we see evil, or the shadow side of life, as the downside of the creative process, we will finally understand that there is *no* evil. What we have thought of as evil is included in omnipotence and omnipresence. Evil is not an illusion. If there is an illusion, it is our *belief that there is a power or presence apart from our higher consciousness.*

Evil is a divine reversal that contains a previously unacceptable secret of life. A "reversal" is a word that when spelled from either end has different meanings, often one that paradoxically contradicts the other. Evil spelled backward becomes "live." Life and evil are two polar ends of one principle. The time has come to end contradiction by recognizing the purpose behind this divinely reversible word.

Without seeing that the words "live" and "evil" are reversals we cannot empower and fulfill our spiritual destiny because we continue to perpetuate contradiction. Once we double-think and see from both ends of the divine telescope, we will know how to turn the telescope around and see a world beyond good and evil where life is a divine process.

In order to understand and accept how evil is a necessary polar aspect of life, we have to realize two things: first, that what we think of as evil is a relative term, and second, what we may believe to be evil in our own personal circumstance may not be so in another's, just as what is beautiful to us may be considered repulsive to others. The minute we judge something as being evil we are involving ourselves with material conditions that are relative and not supported by an eternal or spiritual law. Anything that is supported by divine law cannot be changed – everything else is relative.

We will never become free of evil by telling ourselves that it does not exist or that it has no power, but we will become free if we destroy our old concept of evil as a power apart from the divine process of life. The only way we can do that is to become aware that a creative polarity exists in life that is necessary for the evolution of spiritual growth. In that light there is neither good nor bad but something beyond both that we call God.

Objectively, we all agree that crimes like rape, murder, and brutality are evil. However, to understand how it is possible for something we consider to be evil to be a necessity we have to look at it subjectively, and let enough time pass to see what positive effect eventually became apparent. For instance, when the English empire spread over the whole world, what was considered to be its rape of India was thought by many to be evil, but because of England's domination of India and its far-flung empire, the English language became the universal means of communication, and unless nations communicate we will never have peace on earth.

If we are to simplify and categorize every experience we have as either good or evil, then anything in the dark or shadow side of life, or anything we consider to be evil, as opposed to good, will be listed in the evil column. Anything that is difficult for us to do, anything that is painful, exhausting, undesirable, or aggravating, anything that depletes us, or anything in which it is difficult for us to see good will be included. The point is that unless we can see how the shadow side of life creatively fits into the divine process, there is no way we can believe in omnipotence or omnipresence.

A good example to consider is pain. Pain is thought of as a bad thing, and yet on another level pain has a divine purpose. It lets us know when something is wrong with our bodies, and in that way it serves a creative function. Without the pain, or evil, caused by hunger we would not eat, and without eating we would not live. Destruction is considered evil, and yet there are no creative acts that do not involve some type of destruction. In order to have wood to build a house we have to cut down trees. If we are potters and want to throw a pot, the clay must be ripped from the ground. We have always considered death to be evil and thereby have misunderstood the message of life eternal. We have to die to or face evil daily in order to live – it is the ultimate reversal. If we are honest with ourselves, the majority of us will admit that our most painful experiences became our most valuable times of growth. Through them we matured and became stronger and thus more understanding of the spiritual nature of our lives.

Only by comprehending the part evil, or what we have thought to be evil, plays in our lives can we triumph over our old judgments of evil. What we think of as evil is really a necessary energy, like the negative current in a light bulb that combines with the positive to make the light possible. Everything and every act represent energy. Therefore, subjectively, those things that we feel are difficult, or evil, create the fuel that elicits the positive and energizes living. Difficulty is a necessary part of creativity. It is an energy that spurs us into action, and when we do not think of our difficulties as evil, or powers apart from the process of life, we can transmute that energy into creativity much more quickly and with far less pain.

When I was producing Broadway plays I found at those times when rehearsals went smoothly – when there were no problems and we all got along beautifully – we opened on the road and flopped. On the other hand, when problems showed up in rehearsals, when temperaments clashed and painful changes had to be made, a kind of creative energy came into being and we opened to surprising success.

I don't like having difficult physical or mental experiences pop up in my life any more than you do, but deep inside I know that when they occur what will come out of them represents a kind of necessary creative energy that keeps me growing and fulfilling my purpose for being. I also know that realizing there is an underlying divine principle helps me to transmute those depressing moments into joy with a far greater speed than ever before. Instead of running from evil, I use what looks like evil to motivate me to turn within to my God-source and transmute that necessary energy into a creative purpose. Sometimes I even welcome the rough spots, because they remind me that the energy of life is still flowing through my experiences, transforming dross into gold.

In the second part of the book I will address the "how to's" of handling evil; however, the key to solving our crisis of perception has to do with the energy behind our perception of evil more than any other thing. Changing our perceptions works; it really works. If we can eliminate the small evils by perceiving them in a different way than we have in the past, then the big ones are less likely to occur.

When we center our spirit within our higher consciousness and take our problems and hold them in that place beyond both good and bad, where everything has a divine purpose, their solutions become obvious. We must eliminate any thought or perception of either good or bad. Once we do that, what we thought was good becomes perpetual and the bad loses its sting. They both just *are*.

The Villain "And"

*I*n the second chapter of *Genesis* the "Lord God" led Adam and Eve astray by telling them they should not eat of the tree of the knowledge of good and evil. Good or evil was not the problem; the problem was that old villain "and." As long as we buy into good "and" evil and do not see them as a polarity rather than a duality, we either ignore evil by calling it illusion or we deny omnipotence by accepting evil as a power that emanates apart from the divine.

Unless "and" is accompanied by double-thinking, where both sides of a situation are united, "and" creates the kind of either-or thinking that encourages absolutes and denies the need for complements. "And" divides and conquers, but double-thinking makes it possible to see two sides without division. The good news is that we can consciously do something today that, in general, few could even imagine several decades ago. We can consciously perceive and tune into several different dimensions of a subject at the same time without homogenizing them and losing sight of their individual qualities. By double-thinking we can simultaneously be aware of ourselves as both the observer and that which we are observing.

Some will say that double-thinking makes us a house divided, and they quote the Scripture from James that says, "A double minded man is unstable in all his ways," but the paradox is that, like the two commandments to love God and love neighbor, only by simultaneously including both sides of a situation – the divine and the human – can we arrive at a true unity where we are not a divided consciousness.

Eckhart Tolle had an experience of the spiritual condensate condition where unity is experienced that changed his life and led him to write about it in *The Power Of Now*. In his book he defines what it means to "live in the now." Living in the now is impossible as long as "and" divides time into either-or. It is obvious that we can't have a worry or a fear without thinking in terms of time, either past or future. As long as we think third-dimensionally and see our humanity as other than our divinity, we remain caught in the pairs of opposites where good "and" bad, past "and" future, spiritual "and" material exist.

It is doubtful that one can totally stay in the "now" as long as that person sees him or herself as being a body that is functioning in material time and a self that exists as life eternal. In other words, Jesus was still at the time-continuum-level when he said, "Touch me not, for I have not yet ascended." Though he taught the "now" – that we should "take no thought for the morrow" – he hadn't consistently reached it himself until he arrived at the ascension state of consciousness. When that spiritual condensate was experienced, his physical and spiritual selves became totally one Self without any "and."

Our Blessed Humanity

By the time that I saw the fallacy in either-or and absolute thinking, I had already studied all the world's major religions and had investigated a number of philosophical approaches. I saw that all of them, perhaps with the exception of some of the indigenous ones, had perpetuated a devastating contradiction that up until today has kept us subservient to superstition and makes it impossible for us to close the gap between our selves and our spiritual potential.

All religions are based on there being an ultimate cause, a presence or intelligence underlying our existence that is not only all-powerful but the only power, and at the same time they contradict that premise by teaching us that there are powers we have to overcome. The mystics in all religions claim that we are one "with," if not "as," that presence, yet simultaneously in both the East and the West our theologians have made it impossible for us to experience ourselves as spiritual beings by telling us that our humanity is something we have to get rid of.

Teaching us that we must squelch our humanity in order to be spiritual has been the prime method used to keep the masses subservient to organized religions. Such dogma is a far cry from Jesus' teaching. Religions, in the past and the present, have told us to disown our humanity by hiding it in a monastery or cave, to muzzle it in a mental or philosophical straight-jacket, to subdue it in a man-made morality, and finally to subordinate ourselves to organizations or teachers that tell us how to live and what to think. Others have denied our humanity by claiming that it is an illusion, and many try to escape from it through the use of drugs and alcohol.

In his *The Hymn of The Universe*, Pierre Teilhard de Chardin said, "As the years go by, I come to see more and more clearly, in myself and in those around me, that the great secret preoccupation of modern man is much less to battle for possession of the world than to find a means of escaping from it." Duality has been continuously perpetuated because religions have fallen into the either-or, or "and," trap in two ways – first by not finding a divine purpose for our humanity and then by denying it equal status with our divine nature. Instead of helping us to understand that it is necessary to have a human personality in order to achieve a conscious realization of our divinity, they have degraded our individuality and thus the importance of One.

Even though the metaphysical movement came into being in order to contest the traditional concept of sin and to emphasize our oneness with the divine, it also fell into the either-or trap by saying that the human condition is not included in our reality and by pointing their mental fingers at us while asking "What was in your consciousness that made this awful thing happen?" Without our human experiences, we would not have to face the challenges that make us conscious beings. Without there being human limitations there would be nothing to require our growing into self-realization. Loving our humanity is what awakens us to our spiritual magnificence.

In the Western culture, the most crippling blow to our ability to love ourselves occurred at the Council of Nicea in 325 A.D. At that time Constantine, the emperor of Rome, assembled all the disparate factions of the Christian movement, and by announcing that he would make their religion the official religion of the Roman Empire, he institutionalized and codified the Christian myth. *The Nicean Creed* was created by the Council, and its repetition has become an important ritual in most established churches ever since. Those who say the creed affirm, "I believe in God the Father almighty, creator of heaven and earth, and in his only son, Jesus Christ."

Those who believed that Jesus was the only son of God not only separated heaven from earth, but they almost stifled the spiritual or subjective message inherent in our Judeo-Christian myth. By claiming that Jesus was God's only son they alienated the Jews from the Christians, us individually from ourselves, and Jesus from his humanity, making it impossible for us to believe that he was the same as we are. Not only that, but in doing so they gave us an excuse to ignore his teaching. We could say, "He was God, but I am only human and it's not possible for me to be so perfect."

There is no doubt that Jesus was one of the most inscrutable, dynamic, influential, powerful, and inspirational men the world has ever seen. He transformed nations, spawned a plethora of new philosophies, and personally affected the lives of untold millions. Yet until the Council of Nicea, which was over three hundred years after his death, Jesus was considered to be simply a great teacher and prophet and not God's "only begotten son." By declaring that Jesus was uniquely the presence of God, the church took possession of his identity and used that claim to substantiate its authority. That was one of the ways it held power over its followers.

If the church had emphasized Jesus' humanity – that he stumbled and fell, cried, and even violated some of his own principles – we could more realistically identify with him. If they had taught us that despite his human frailties Jesus triumphed over material limitation, we could look at our own humanity in a different way, and we could have taken his teachings even more seriously. If instead of always trying to compare our human feelings with what the divine Jesus felt we could compare his humanity with ours. We would then better understand that we too can triumph over any obstacle, even death, just as he did.

Except on one occasion, Jesus referred to himself as the "son of man," which in Old Testament language means "human." By repeatedly saying the equivalent of "I'm human, I'm human," and by also asserting that he was one with the divine, he was trying to tell us that we as humans were the same as he.

Jesus was perfect, but not flawless. He was all that a perfectly evolving, growing, learning, human being is supposed to be, just as you and I are. In coping with his own shortcomings he developed the principles that we profit from today. He didn't die for us in the self-sacrificing way we have been taught, but by demonstrating the truths that he had discovered during his own human struggle, our lives are better.

Transcending Obsolescence

Our current evolutionary advances have made the past obsolete – not valueless, but obsolete. Every lesson we have learned has been necessary in order to get us to this point, but to participate in the shift that is taking place in the world's consciousness today, we have to have the strength to let go of what worked for us in the past, no matter how time-tested and infallible it seems.

Keep in mind that every stage of consciousness has been right for its time. All of us are right on schedule in terms of our own spiritual evolutions, and that applies individually for everyone who has ever existed. No matter what church, synagogue, or mosque one does or does not attend, no matter what path one follows, no matter what values one currently lives by, everything that one is experiencing represents exactly where that person should be in the process of his or her own spiritual evolution.

In this geometrically speeded-up time, there are attitudes and beliefs that were right for us in the very recent past that have become obsolete for us today, and to hang on to them because they worked successfully in the past might assure today's failures. To update our thinking we must first see the virtue in what we have considered to be verifiable truths in the past before we can see that, though true, they have become half-truths that must be added to other half-truths in order to be today's whole truth. Until recognized half-truths are complemented by other half-truths, we unwittingly confuse ourselves. Until the purpose of our humanity is united with the truth of our divinity, unintentional contradiction complicates our actions.

In the past we thought it was a spiritual virtue for us to arrive at the place where we wanted to be "channels" for God. We didn't realize that as long as we think of ourselves as being channels, we are creating the duality we sought to eliminate. When we perceive ourselves as channels there are two – ourselves and whatever it is that we are channeling. If we think that way, it shows that we are still seeing ourselves in terms of half-truths, as nouns. We are simultaneously both channels and that which is being channeled.

Another superstition we often hear people unintentionally perpetuate is that "God is with us." How many times have you been told to believe that? Wrong! God is not an object that is with another object (us) – *God is appearing as us.* God is not with us as though there are two separate beings present; God is our presence being present. And what about that "in" word? If we believe that God is "in" us, we continue to see ourselves as nouns that have some other thing occupying us. We are both that which is in us and that which takes form as our bodies. *As long as we believe that God is in us, we are still seeing God as an object that can be somewhere else and is other than ourselves.*

At times I still find myself saying that God is "in" me or "with" me, and when I do I remind myself that I have fallen back into thinking of myself objectively as a body. When I once more double-think, I remember that my consciousness is me, and that God is my consciousness. The truth of being is included in my consciousness. The "withs" and the "ins" are appearing "as" me. Another half-truth that is becoming obsolete is our concept of what it means to do God's will. As long as we think in terms of wanting to do God's will, we separate ourselves from our own divinity by believing that there are two wills, ours and God's. In that case, we are still seeing ourselves strictly as physical beings.

Even some of those people who do not see themselves or label themselves in terms that relate to religions make the same mistake as those who do have religious references. Anyone, religious or not, who thinks that there is a creative source or outside influence other than that which is included as his or her own being is indulging in the same dualistic thinking that is ultimately entertained by religious extremists. To the degree that they impose limitation on themselves, so called "existentialists" also see themselves as finite beings separate from life's process. They create the same duality as those who believe God is somewhere off in space. As long as there is a sense of self "and" something else, to that degree division insinuates itself into one's consciousness.

The divine process is active everywhere as omnipresence; it includes infinite knowledge as omniscience, and its nature is the one creative energy of omnipotence. If that is accepted as fact then that omnipresence is sitting in your chair, wearing your clothes, breathing your air. In fact, it "is" your chair, your clothes, and the air you breathe. It and you do not exist separately. Separation is a mentally perceived illusion. You are infinite consciousness individually expressing itself in a finite way without any "and."

Chapter 4

The Third Appearance

*I*n order for you to understand and personally experience what I refer to as the spiritual condensate, I have outlined a few imperatives. We must see ourselves as consciousness rather than form, we must get rid of the superstitious belief that there is a God apart from our own being, and we must recognize the divinity of our humanity. We must also develop the capacity to consciously double-think, and go beyond believing in the duality of good and evil. When those conditions have been met we will witness the Third Appearance of God and realize that it is us – it is our individual selves and humanity as a whole.

When the concept of *The Third Appearance* first crystallized itself in my awareness, I thought, "Walter, now you have gone too far." However, as I became increasingly aware of the alarming inevitabilities being anticipated by some of our scientists, I felt obligated to write this book alerting others, as well as myself, to take personal responsibility for our part in what is taking place. I believe that the survival of the human race literally depends on our recognizing that we are indeed the Third Appearance.

Return for a moment to the truth symbolized by our Judeo-Christian myth. Whether fact or fiction, one man two-thousand-years-ago claimed equality with God, and the world worshiped him for embodying it. They honored him not because of his miraculous resurrection experience; they were drawn to his story because they sensed that through the process of spiritual evolution that is taking place, all of us will eventually arrive at the same high point of consciousness that he had attained.

For many years I circled around the idea that humankind is how God appears in the human scene. I had divided the evolution of our conscious awareness of God, or our arrival at the God experience, into three stages. The first stage was objective – where humanity perceived God objectively as a supreme being apart from and other than humankind. The second stage was both objective and subjective – appearing objectively as the man Jesus and subjectively as a state of consciousness known as the Christ. The third stage eliminates all duality as human beings realize that they are the very presence of God.

A few years ago, my evolutionary concept was further confirmed in Biblical terms by my reading *The Disappearance of God* by Dr.. Richard Friedman. Friedman received his degree of Doctor of Theology at Harvard and was a visiting scholar at Oxford and Cambridge. He is an honored Bible scholar and is currently a Professor of Hebrew at the University of California, San Diego.

Like myself, Friedman believes that we face an awesome responsibility in the new millennium. To substantiate his conclusions, using detailed examples, he carefully and brilliantly delineates the evolution of our concepts of God. He shows how at the beginning of the Old Testament God was not only visible and personal to human beings but he was also heard in explicit and audible ways. Friedman writes, "In the first few chapters of the

Bible, God is utterly involved in the affairs of the first humans." His text pictures God and humans in a state of intimacy that is unmatched in subsequent Biblical narratives.

The beginnings of a split between God and human beings appears in Genesis when Adam and Eve refuse to follow his orders. Eventually Moses places a veil over God by claiming that only he can see God. Moses also takes an independent step that causes an alienation between the Old Testament concept of God and man. The Israelites need water and God tells Moses to speak to a stone so that water will come forth, but Moses performs the act in his own way. He strikes the stone with his rod. The water comes forth, and Moses then implies that he is responsible for the miracle. Moses' feat represents the initial step that a human being takes, implying that human beings are equal to God.

Friedman goes on to list the countless miracles that God performs throughout most of the Old Testament. God destroys whole nations, defeats great armies, and demonstrates total power over humankind. But as time goes on God becomes less and less available, until by the end of the Old Testament there are no more miracles attributed to God, and less mention of God at all. If anything, by the end, God becomes more a social phenomenon than a miracle worker. Finally the Old Testament God disappears altogether. That concludes Friedman's first appearance of God.

As I see it, that Old Testament God is a personal-sense God, one that appeals to those who can only relate to things objectively in materially identifiable terms. In actuality, that concept of God represents the belief in the presence of God as a kind of super or supreme being, a father figure keeping score and handing down punishment.

The second appearance of God takes place in the New Testament. This time God appears in the flesh as a man, a human being who is both objective - the physical Jesus – and subjective – as the Christ consciousness. This second appearance God-man, who is both divine and human, also performs godly miracles similar to those in the Old Testament. He raises the dead, heals the blind, and feeds the multitudes by mysteriously multiplying the loaves and fishes, but, complemented by his subjective nature, he heals the masses rather than destroying them as the Old Testament God had sometimes done. The disappearing act continues, and by the end of the Gospels this God-man also visibly disappears in order to prepare us for the next and current collective re-appearance of God that I call the Third Appearance.

If we carefully read his words, we will see that Jesus advocated a different priority than the Old Testament's "an eye for an eye and a tooth for a tooth." He didn't deny a place for the objective approach and the need to at times think of God as "Father"; however, he clearly stated that objective goals wouldn't work unless subjective values preceded objective actions. By saying, "seek ye first the kingdom of God," Jesus made the subjective concept of God primary.

By the end of the Gospels the purely objective physical Jesus presence had served its purpose in our spiritual evolution and, though still a valuable viewpoint, Jesus will now be seen primarily as a metaphor for the Christ-consciousness that has prepared us to become the Third Appearance.

The 21ˢᵗ Century Revelation

I have written, and a number of other metaphysicians have said, that the so-called "second coming of Christ" would not be a reappearance of a man with Christ-consciousness, but, rather, that it would be the advent of that illumined Christ state of consciousness appearing in humankind as a whole. If so, the Third Appearance is not only now being recognized by the collective consciousness, but it is also being experienced individually by you and me. Consciously or subconsciously, the Apostle Paul was being prophetic when he said "Let this mind be in you, which was also in Christ Jesus: Who, being in the form of God, thought it not robbery to be equal with God…"

The revelation that we are the Third Appearance becomes more than an intellectual exercise when we look at the evidence. Collectively, many of the incredible things that we human beings are now doing would have been attributed only to God in the past. We are cloning human beings, we have mapped the entire gene code making it possible to alter our lives and bodies in every conceivable way, and through stem cell research we will soon be able to grow new limbs on our bodies if we need to. We can move five times faster than the speed of sound. And, as I predicted earlier, through advances in nanotechnology we will soon be able to build life forms and new organs for our bodies atom by atom.

If humans are now responsible for what were thought in the past to be God's miracles, what does that tell us? It tells us that we individually have the power to create anything we can conceive of. The revelation is crystal clear: we can do anything we want to do, but with this creative power comes responsibility. As Einstein said, "The world we have created is a product of our way of thinking."

For the first time in the history of the world we have created a runaway technology with the power to destroy life on earth as we know it, and we will do so if we do not take responsibility – individually and collectively – for consciously being the presence of God.

I used to say that we might destroy life on earth rather than destroy life as we know it until someone pointed out to me that even after the demise of the dinosaurs, life not only continued but continued in an even more advanced way. Life will go on no matter what we do, but we human beings won't be a part of it unless we take responsibility for being the Third Appearance and begin to use our technology with more altruistic goals.

At present we are polluting our environment and punching holes in the ozone layer, destroying our rain forests, poisoning our oceans, ravishing our natural resources, and dumping radioactive waste into the land. Personally, we are filling our bodies with drugs and alien substances with no concern for their long-range side effects and bombarding ourselves with an overload of sensual impact through our addiction to the media.

The fact that more and more individuals are taking responsibility for being the Gods we are destined to be is not accidental. Those who support the Sierra Club, fund humanitarian relief groups, sit in trees to stop their slaughter; those who are helping to stamp out AIDS, voting their conscience, and making their voices heard, are individually taking responsibility for personally being the presence of God. Public gatherings and marches on our capitols are made up of people who feel it is their place to demand justice for all human beings. People in nations all over the globe are joining together to turn their thoughts and meditations toward sending out the message of peace. On World Water Day 2000, a forum meeting in The Hague made a commitment to see that every person on earth has access to enough safe water. Those are all signs of individuals taking responsibility for being the presence of God.

Through our evolving understanding we are getting there subjectively, but it won't happen objectively until each one of us individually accepts his or her divine destiny and actually experiences the presence of God in and as themselves.

We may already be activists, but until we have individually experienced the presence of God as our very own being, we cannot be as effective as we must be. This is where the mystical teachings of all ages and cultures come in. As long as humans have existed, our mystics have told us that it is possible for us to actually experience ourselves as one with God. Secret societies, such as the Masons, identify themselves by the name, "I AM." At the beginning of the Old Testament Moses was given the commission, I AM THAT I AM, and Jesus voiced the truth of each of us when he said, "I AM the way, the truth, and the life." Our task now, if freedom is to become a reality, is to understand how we can consciously experience ourselves as the Third Appearance of God and reconcile that with our personal or individual presence as human beings. It has always been true that everyone is individually one with and as the divine, but not having the conscious awareness and experience of it has made it impossible for us to demonstrate that truth. In other words, our freedom will not come because of our relationship with God; *it will come because of our conscious awareness and experience of the fact that we are the Third Appearance.*

It may take a while for our nations to assume responsibility for the use of our technology because nations are like individuals, they don't change until they have to. Perhaps ecological changes will be the collective trigger. But I know, with all the fiber of my being as well as from my years of observation, that what's happening now is a blessed wake-up call, and it is right on time as part of a grand design. If we take responsibility now for being the presence of God, we can stop the misuse of our creative consciousness and turn this world into what we have always thought heaven to be.

When I wrote *The Gospel of Relativity* some thirty years ago, I had no idea how accurately prophetic the story about the end of the world that I began the book with would be. However, I concluded the story with a happy ending, and when we resolve our present crisis it will be the same today. We will meet this challenge, because in the end we will collectively perceive of ourselves as the presence of God on earth, and we will accept individual responsibility for ourselves, for nature, and for the world.

The Third Appearance is that moment when God and man are fused into one being.

Conscious Being

*I*n the fifteenth century people were burned at the stake for saying or even implying that they were God or one with God. If those today who primarily see themselves as nouns, as personalities, were to personally claim to be God, they would be just as worthy of denunciation. Every few years we see examples of charismatic personalities, such as the Branch Davidian leader David Koresh, who mistakenly encourage their followers to believe that their physical presence is exclusively God.

The tyrants and dictators that have caused such havoc in the world over the past hundred years are examples of individuals who have had a vision of themselves as being the presence of God; however, they have mistakenly identified that feeling with personal sense. By the same token, it would be a foolhardy mistake for any of us to go around telling others that we are God as long as we still think we are primarily what we see in the mirror. Anyone who feels the need to say that he or she is the presence of God, isn't.

It is unlikely that anyone who has experienced his or

her higher consciousness, the I AM of their self, would publicly make the statement, "I am God," because they would not want to confuse others with a half-truth. They would be aware that their human appearance was only a finite symbol of their consciousness and not the full, infinite, nature of self that is God. Those who can see their identity or physical presence as a vehicle in the service of their divine consciousness, as the livingness of their presence, could legitimately claim to be God or an individual expression of God-consciousness in the presence of those who would understand what they are talking about, but not otherwise.

Spiritual evolution has brought us to the place where it is now possible to double-think and know that when we say we are God we are talking about ourselves as cause appearing as effect – as verbs appearing as nouns. We can be both objectively aware of our physical selves and consciously aware of being the life force that is activating our lives. Without confusing our egos with our divine purpose in life, this frees us to take our place as the presence of God.

To believe that our materialized human self cannot be seen as our God-presence denies God's omnipresence. Such a one-dimensional way of looking at life creates the very ignorance it believes it is trying to eliminate. Perhaps it would be more understandable if instead of saying, "I am God," we were to say, "God is that which I am."

I used to cringe when I heard ministers proclaim, "Jesus is Lord." I don't any more because I realize that any man who could say, "I am the way, the truth, and the life," knew he was the spirit, or consciousness, that was living in or as his body. If it is the truth about him, it must also be the truth about you and me. We will see that we are all God once we realize that we are the life force that animates our existence.

The Waves and the Ocean

*U*ntil we understand the subjective nature of ourselves and experience it objectively as our personal physical presence, we are doing no more than playing with words. In order to do so, we have to understand how the finite relates to the infinite, and that is not easy to accomplish.

We must of necessity begin by realizing and experiencing the importance of our individual and finite selves. That single realization is similar to the carburetor in an automobile. Without that workable part, a top-of-the-line car is no more than a piece of junk unable to fulfill its purpose. The five-pound carburetor is as important to successful transportation as the five-thousand-pound automobile.

Another example is the relationship between an individual wave and the ocean. It is obvious that an individual wave cannot exist without an ocean in which to exist. Though each finite wave has all of the elements of the ocean within it, the infinite ocean is more extensive than the wave. Nevertheless, each individual wave is as important as the ocean itself since without any waves there wouldn't be an ocean. They are equally dependent on each other.

In the Gospel of John we are told that we are like branches that wither and die if they are cut off from the vine. What we are not told is that the vine cannot exist without branches. The branches give life to the vine and bears its fruit. When we think of ourselves as less than or other than both the vine and the branches, we cut ourselves off from condensate consciousness where the vine and its branches are one.

Jesus was establishing unity when he said, "I and my Father are One, but the Father is greater than I." However, unless his words as quoted in the Bible were mistranslated, there is a contradiction in his statement. In "Oneness" there is no superior or inferior. Perhaps he meant, "I [my subjective concept of self] and my Father [my God Self] are one, but my Father is 'larger' or more all-encompassing than I [my personal self]." In that way one aspect is no better than the other, whether referring to the human and the divine or to our objective and subjective selves.

I believe the progress of spiritual evolution didn't stop with Jesus. When he said, "Greater works than these shall ye do," he was announcing that those who followed him would further push the envelope of consciousness. Today we are becoming conscious of the fact that humankind is as important to God as God is to humankind. They are one and the same. While this theory may be a shock to traditional religionists, it is the foundation belief that supports the Third Appearance.

Consciousness is God. There has never been a God other than consciousness, and in humankind consciousness has become conscious of itself. Humankind is the high point of the evolution of consciousness. Man is God's recognition of Himself. Humankind is creative consciousness embodied. When rational thought fueled by imagination evolved in Homo Sapiens, their ability to create new forms or destroy old ones became a conscious act. Consciousness has evolved since it appeared as the first one-cell amoebas, and it will continue to do so. That means God is growing, and we, as God's presence, will continue to grow.

When I said previously that we humans are now affecting our own evolution, I wasn't talking about us as physical beings. I was saying that as consciousness expressing itself in form it becomes obvious that we humans are collectively the dominant Godly influence in the world. Quantum physicists tell us that for anything to exist there has to be someone conscious of it. From this day on we cannot exist without consciously recognizing that our higher consciousness is the presence of God, and God cannot exist except through and as that state of consciousness we are. We are the presence of God.

Until we accept as fact that even with our human shortcomings we are individually the Third Appearance, we will continue to maintain a sense of inferiority and it will be impossible for us to experience the spiritual condensate. We must consciously experience and know something now that many will consider utter blasphemy – that apart from the consciousness that expresses itself as humankind there is no other God!

Perception precedes actuality. Within each and every one of us is the potential to be all that God is. If we perceive it as fact, that potential will begin to manifest itself in stages until we find ourselves free of self-imposed limitation. *We are the consciousness of God, and God is the consciousness we are.* When we double-think and see our lives existing as a polarity between the finite and the infinite, we will no longer confuse the two ends of the spectrum. We will have solved the "crisis of perception" and become the Third Appearance. We will have grown up.

Recognized Potential

*T*o grow up is to fulfill our potential. When we came into the world we expected our fathers and mothers to feed and protect us, to guide and discipline us, and to love us. As we grew we were taught to seek these things from a supreme being, and we went to that God expectantly in the same way that children go to their parents to have their needs fulfilled. The time eventually came in our lives when to realize our potential as adults we had to go out into the world and stand on our own two feet. Now we must stand on our own God-representative higher consciousness.

We must no longer look outside of ourselves, but rather to that which we are – God's presence on earth. That is our destiny and our responsibility. We must respond to the God that is appearing as us and no longer deny that we are made in the image of that God. If, in our insecure human moments, we have to turn to something for support, let us turn to our own higher consciousness.

What I am saying isn't new. Freud also compared the accepting of our responsibility to be our higher selves with what we face as children when we have to break with dependence on our parents. He wrote:

> *They [the grown children] will have to admit to themselves the full extent of their helplessness [at the ego level] and their insignificance in the machinery of the universe; they can no longer be the center of creation, no longer the object of tender care on the part of a beneficent Providence. They will be in the same position as a child who has left the parent's house where he was so warm and comfortable. But surely infantilism is destined to be surmounted. Men cannot remain children forever.*

Most of the turmoil the world has already experienced in the opening days of the twenty-first century has been taking place because we are in the process of being kicked out of our old homes – our old state of consciousness. The ultimate purpose is to force us to make a home for ourselves in divine consciousness.

This, again, is why for now we must consciously double-think and be at home in both identities, both the self we are growing out of and our ultimate potential. If we can be simultaneously aware of both, we can know ourselves in a godly way without becoming egotistical or self-deluded. By double-thinking we can consciously stand aside and observe our own individual vehicle-selves without being overwhelmed by a sense of responsibility. With this double-sense we can be realistic about our human limitation while retaining our awareness of being the presence of God.

When enough of us have resolved the crisis of perception, we will have reversed the old priority that says we are first humans and secondarily divine beings, and see ourselves primarily as God's presence instead of seeing ourselves as limited physical beings. When the wave ceases to think of itself as just a wave and sees itself as how the ocean appears at the finite level, it is ready to take responsibility for being the ocean.

The Age of Responsibility

The time has come for us to accept our responsibility for taking full control of our lives and for us to accept the mutual interdependence of our human and spiritual existences. There is no turning back. Old paradigms, like placing our faith in a power apart from our own higher consciousness, will no longer work for us. They were appropriate for their stage of our evolution, but they will work in reverse once we have witnessed the spiritual condensate level of consciousness. We can desperately try to hang on to our old perceptions, our old concepts, but we will eventually self-destruct if we do.

In the twenty-first century we can no longer use God as an excuse for our limitations. We can no longer light a candle or say a prayer to an entity outside of our own being as though anything or anyone beyond our individual control could or would come to our aid. We cannot have it both ways. *Either we are as Jesus claimed, one and the same as God, thus heirs to all that we have thought God to be, or we are not. The only God that will act in our lives is our own Selves, with a capital "S."*

Evolution, by its very nature, does not present us with a difficulty to overcome without also giving us the solution and the strength to overcome it. Even though we may try to avoid our responsibility, the problems our society faces will not go away until we actively apply the consciousness of truth. Once we have recognized the truth and voiced it, we must then act it out. We must honor the earth and nurture it. We must perceive the wholeness of the bodies, minds, and spirits of the people we come in contact with because they are extensions of our own oneness. We must let go of any conditions or beliefs that are exclusive, or of selfish interest because "they" are "we," and we are God.

Responsibility begins at home, but home is not a place, it is the consciousness in which we live. We must respond to the world of appearances and all that comes into our consciousness right where we are. Responsibility in no way deprives us of the magic and awe we had when we believed in a God apart from ourselves. The realization that potentially each of us is all that God is is just as awe-inspiring as ever before. To be anointed is to respond to that awe, the awe of self-love.

Once we take responsibility for being the divine presence that we are, our dominion over the world of effects follows. It may take years for the old habits of thought, the old lack of self-love, the old sense of limitation to be dissolved; but when they are discarded we will realize that we are life eternal, without any limitations.

The Holy Instant

*M*ost of the time we walk around feeling like human beings, but at infinitely brief moments we can experience who we really are – *humans appearing as the presence of God.* In meditation, or at any time that personal sense is put aside, a "holy instant" can happen. Those are the fleeting moments when we experience our higher consciousness – the spiritual condensate where the divine and the human merge. Though instantaneous, the light that comes through during those moments of contact can change our lives as well as the world.

In Plato's cave analogy he claimed that what we see are the shadows on the wall cast by the light, but that if we were to look straight at the light it would burn our eyes out. Perhaps that was true in Plato's day, but we have now spiritually evolved to the point where we can experience a holy instant, and for a brief moment we can look right at the light. We can even become the light itself. It is amazing how those instant flashes of higher consciousness can transform our lives, our negative encounters, and even our world. Those holy instances not only place us under a new and more divine set of laws, but when they happen we are given instructions on what to do; we have access to incredible energy, and we are led in meaningful directions.

If enough of us experience condensate we will become a critical mass that will transform our world. That isn't because there is a God somewhere keeping tally and rewarding our righteousness. It is because our collective consciousness becomes a transformative energy.

Long ago, military leaders learned not to march armies in cadence across bridges. When they came to a bridge they would stop marching and have the soldiers walk across the bridge independently. They found that if the soldiers marched in unison a vibration built up that would shake the bridge off its foundations.

When enough of us think the same thoughts, have the same vision, believe in the same truths, and march in unison, a vibration will build up that will shake old beliefs and obsolete social structures from their foundation. One person alone cannot do it, nor can a group acting individually. But if enough of us who are willing to accept the responsibility of being the presence of God, the Third Appearance, move together at the same time then we won't be just ten righteous men saving a city, but rather a multitude that saves nations and ultimately the world. The collective consciousness energy of human beings in unison can move mountains.

The Age of Nations is past.
The Task before us now,
if we would not perish,
is to build the earth.
Pierre Teilard de Chardin

Part Two

Chapter 5

The Fabric of Consciousness

*I*t is one thing for me to announce boldly that we humans are the Third Appearance of God; it is quite another matter for me to humanly accompany that noetic assumption with meaningful and practical examples of how we can individually fulfill that promise.

The reason I have split this book into two parts is simple. In the first part of the book I addressed the subjective viewpoint about the "what" of our lives. I talked about the impersonal, divine sense of self with the intention of suggesting concepts that would make it possible for us to then observe ourselves as the presence of God. In this second part of the book, I am proposing ways that include different threads of consciousness, which, when consciously woven together, make up the fabric of our divine-human lives.

Each thread, no matter how seemingly unimportant, is needed; however, the value lies in the fact that woven together the various threads lay the groundwork for an experience of the condensate state of consciousness. I ask that you be aware of the consciousness that lies between the lines, and withhold judgment until the multifaceted tapestry of consciousness is complete.

Walter and I

*U*ntil I had an actual experience of the condensate state of consciousness, my old concepts of spirituality remained as mentally papered-over theories. The transition from theory to practice was not an automatic process. I had to individually find directions that would result in experiences that would make it happen for me. The individual examples I am offering are of themselves unimportant, but the consciousness they illustrate is. Collectively, they illustrate my graduation to a level of consciousness that has made it possible for me to experience a more consistent awareness of my higher self. When I refer to myself as Walter, I am talking about my personal sense of self, the one I see in the mirror, and what he has gone through in his progression.

On those days when Walter is feeling inadequate, insecure, or judgmental, he wonders if he is not a spiritual *Man of La Mancha*, insanely implying that he or anyone else can fulfill "the impossible dream" – the Third Appearance. On the other hand, in those brief moments when Walter gets out of the way, I know without a doubt that I'm on the right track. Tilting at windmills or not, all of us must take responsibility for resolving our present crisis of perception, and I am personally willing to do whatever it takes. The impossible dream is no longer a dream. It's an emerging and necessary reality, and the time has come to recognize it.

As Walter, I live in a state of free-fall, where there is nothing mental or physical to hang on to and where change is a constant way of life. In that state there are certain things I must do. At times I must consciously and deliberately stand aside and observe my own individuality from an objective viewpoint, almost as though my Walter-self is an actor playing a part in a soap opera that I am watching. There are ancient teachings based on the assumption that the observer and the observed are two separate beings, but those teachings are no longer valid. In order to eliminate duality, we have to consciously see ourselves as being simultaneously both divine and human, and be aware of how those two selves relate to each other.

When I stand aside and look at Walter objectively, without trying to fit his personality or actions into a pre-conceived mold, I can see that there is no way he can evaluate or arrive at a spiritually logical explanation for what is happening to him. That's because there is no way Walter can know what his soul needs – if he knew what he needed, he wouldn't need it. There is no way, as a human being, that Walter can recognize the catalytic nature of the spiritual chemistry that speeds his evolution. He may think he is able to, but there is no way he can know when the time has come to dissolve old paradigms or create new ones, take characters out of the script or introduce additional ones, change focus or re-focus. It's a waste of time for Walter to try.

There is also no way Walter can know what stages of evolution other people are going through, or what experiences are necessary for them to stimulate their growth. He can only discover that for himself, and remind himself of it on those occasions when he is tempted to judge the actions of others.

Walter questions, senses change, and has bouts of anxiety, though fewer than in the past. Walter would like to know what's in store for him in this big shift in the world that he feels is so obviously at hand, and how it will affect his own future. Walter even thinks he cares what happens. Nevertheless, overriding anything that Walter feels, his higher consciousness-self has such a strong and abiding trust in the divine process that even Walter faces the future with confidence and excitement. During those times when he stops trying to figure things out and keeps his focus on his own essential being, he wonders why he ever felt any anxiety at all.

The reason Walter can't figure out what his soul requires of him is because the divine process has never been nor can it be defined intellectually. There is no set pattern for the evolution of a soul. Grace doesn't work that way, and by grace – the divine plan – each of us can take comfort in the realization that we are all uniquely experiencing exactly what is necessary for our soul's evolution.

The substance of our experiences contains different kinds, qualities, and degrees of transformative energy. We have no way of knowing what it is in those experiences that is needed to energize our transformations. To even try is to resist free-fall. The best we can do when we are tempted to psychoanalyze the process is to smile and abandon ourselves to it with love and self-appreciation. The sooner we do, the sooner our intuition will reveal what the experience is trying to tell us, and we can move on to enlightenment.

When I finally learned that my perceptions created my reality and well-being, I realized that I had to accept and maintain the belief that no matter what situations appeared in my life there was an omnipotent power for good operating in it. Even if it did not look that way, if I could perceive that a negative situation could turn out in my favor, it would end up doing so, and to an extraordinary and undeniable extent, it always has. Seemingly disastrous situations have, almost without exception, reversed themselves and have in the end been to my advantage. The break-up of a malfunctioning business partnership freed me to become involved in a highly successful one. The death of a loved one resulted in a whole new and exciting way of life that would not otherwise have taken place.

I finally accepted that because there are no two situations exactly alike, it is impossible for me, as Walter, to understand the relative nature of life. Although Walter is not always at his highest level of awareness, his higher consciousness is nevertheless the controlling power in his life. All Walter has to do is to trust the process.

Because I believe that there is a divine process in my life, that belief has become a self-created perception. In turn, that perception continues to manifest a self-created reality, a reality that isn't dependent on any outside influence or on a God somewhere outside of myself that I must appease. I may doubt Walter at times, but I always trust that my higher consciousness will dictate the result of Walter's endeavors.

Once I stopped trying to figure out whether Walter should take steps to change a circumstance or not, seek a new relationship or not, continue an old one or not, or make a move or not, clouds of indecision were replaced by the gift of obvious and rewarding direction. I knew I had to take actions, but my actions were designed to aid the process rather than to redesign it. "Trust the process," became my motto. The process is right on time, and it doesn't end for any of us until we fulfill our purpose for existing and we reach ascension consciousness.

At this point, most of us are in transit between our old concept of a limited personal self and our awakening to an unlimited life knowingly lived through the recognition of our impersonal, higher divine consciousness. That is why we have no choice but to continue to discover new ways to expose old contradictions and to more consistently live from a subjective approach rather than the old objective or traditional morality.

How you perceive yourself is how you are, present tense, and the crisis of perception is not concluded until your perception of yourself as the Third Appearance becomes a self-fulfilled prophecy.

The New Me

*O*ver the past eighty-plus years I've gone through many deaths and resurrections, as we all have. Every time I've died to an old belief and had the slightest change of consciousness I have become a different self, a different tapestry, than the one I was before, and after each subsequent resurrection I have had, to some extent, to rediscover myself. Often my resurrections have been more confusing and even more painful than my crucifixion experiences. After a resurrection I appear outwardly to be the same person that I was, but inside I am quite different. My spiritual experiences define my inner being; therefore, after changes occur it takes me some time to understand and get used to the new person into which I have evolved.

Both our individual and collective consciousness is currently being transformed so rapidly that we must constantly re-examine who we think we are at the moment and re-evaluate how we expect to operate in today's world. As long as someone identifies with personal sense, that person can't accurately and honestly say, "I know me, and this is the way I am." We are all so much more than we humanly see ourselves as being. After the slightest change in consciousness we are to some extent a new person. To believe that we will know how we will react to situations in the future ignores the effect that the current shift in the collective consciousness is having upon us. Look back to who you were before and after past major crises have taken place in your life, and you will see that afterwards you were not quite the same person. For example, none of us were unaffected and quite the same after September 11, 2001.

Many of us are like actors who have been in a long run of a play and suddenly find ourselves in a new production with a new script. It is difficult for us to shed the habitual responses that were appropriate for the old character we were playing in order for us to be the new one. We keep trying to play the new part in the same way that we would have played it if we were still the old character, but it doesn't work.

To further complicate matters, we are like actors in a stock company who play many different parts at one time or another. As Shakespeare said many years ago, "All the world's a stage, and all the men and women merely players." Those other selves that we have inhabited in the past are still in our repertoires, and it is difficult for us to clearly identify who we are being at present. At times we lapse back into our old states of consciousness, our outdated selves, and we do not always perform as the self that is new to us.

If you are someone who, for no obvious reason that you can explain, is feeling uncomfortable in your occupation, your personal associations, and the lifestyle that you were happy with in the recent past, don't despair. Every time that has happened to me it has signaled the introduction of an important, creative time in my life. When I experienced an inner disquiet it was because I had not yet discovered my new role in life, a role suitable to my newly emerging level of consciousness. Although sometimes it meant moving into a whole new lifestyle or making a break with current associations, that wasn't always the case. Most often, it was time for me to play my part in a new way, and discover a new purpose behind my current personal relationships - perhaps even see how they, too, were changing in a creative way. In other words, my friends, loved ones, and I were all in the process of reinventing ourselves, and in each instance, I had to let go of old opinions and be prepared to go wherever the new "me" took me.

As I look back at those changes, I realize that often after I experienced a more advanced level of consciousness, things and relationships that were comfortable and relevant for me at the old level no longer felt right. I did not want to turn my back on them, but I just didn't feel they belonged in my life anymore. The recognition that change was taking place was the beginning of authority, of authoring or creating a new script for the next stage of my evolution. I soon discovered that my problem was that I couldn't know or outline what was to be in the script until it had happened. The best thing I could do was to stop struggling for a spiritual answer and simply continue to *trust the process*. I knew that though it was wrong for me to try to yank doors open, it would be worse for me if I did not at least investigate the doors that did open to see what I would find.

In order to bring the new "me" into focus, it helped for me to follow the Einstein approach. He worked backward from success, as though it had already been achieved, to the starting point. Rather than trying to resist or overcome obstacles that stood in my way, I tried to find ways to use them to help me succeed.

I looked at life through the "now" end of the telescope rather than the "will be" future. Instead of trying to figure out what to do from the standpoint of my past limitations, I put those old inadequate images aside and created a likeness of the divine-human that I could now see myself being. I found that when I successfully believed in and accepted the new, unlimited person

I had become, I could deal with the obstructions or roadblocks of the past in a positive way. There is no more powerful "how" to solve the crisis of perception than to perceive goals as having already been successfully accomplished.

The Realized "I"

When I am discouraged with my progress, a helpful scripture often comes to mind which says for me to be confident that "he which hath begun a good work in you will perform it until the day of Jesus Christ" (Phil. 1:6). "The day of Jesus Christ" symbolizes the day when the human and the divine are reconciled. At first I thought that the "good work" Paul was talking about referred to some job or project that I was working on. But I finally came to realize that it meant that an automatic evolutionary process was lifting me into a state of consciousness that was greater than my old consciousness, one that was bringing me closer to an awareness of the divine-human that I would soon be prepared to recognize and accept as myself.

Who was the "he" that had begun a good work in me and would perform it until the day when I would become a "Walter Christ" – a human integrated with his higher consciousness? It was I. Though I might have felt more comfortable if I could have believed that there was a supreme being, a kind of heavenly boss who was in charge of my destiny, it didn't work that way for me. Something within me told me that there wasn't any God separate from my own higher self that was doing it; so that "he" that was doing the good work had to stand for another me than my Walter sense of self.

That other self is the self that the mystics refer to as the "I AM." It is the self that the first capitalized letters in the Bible announce: "I AM THAT I AM." When personality is left out of the picture, one's I AM is the recognition of one's unconditioned or essential being.

The ego is one's sense of self. The original root meaning of ego is simply "I," an awareness of self. Egotism is a distortion of the ego; it is what happens when one attributes self-possessed qualities to his or her ego. Descartes defined the ego as "the soul or an underlying mental or spiritual substance." Kant called ego "A transcendentally postulated unity of perception. The consciousness of an individual's being in distinction of other selves." *Webster's Third New International Dictionary* defines the ego as "the self especially as inside one as contrasted with something outside." In simpler terms, the ego is one's sense of his or her invisible being. It is the God in us identified individually as our essential being.

The word "essential" comes from the Latin *essentia* meaning "to be." Its root meaning is "The intrinsic fundamental internal nature of something." Another interpretation is "Absolute, complete, perfect, and pure." In abstract terms, "essential" stands for existence itself. This pure unconditioned essential existence is the I AM. It is all-inclusive; therefore it is impersonal. It is impersonal because it is not just in any one person, but it is the same in every person just waiting to be recognized and experienced. The I AM, or our essential being, is no more or no less than the recognition and experience of our own impersonal existential nature.

The glue that unites the divine and the human into the one Self is the I AM. When I, as Walter, actually experienced that impersonal universal nature as my Self, it was one of the most profound turning points in my life. That realization made it possible for me to stand aside and be objective about my personal self from an impersonal viewpoint.

The reason it is so difficult for any of us to personally feel that this divine revelation is our own individual self is precisely because it is impersonal. You can't grasp it with your personal intellect. Yet, when your ego is off-guard and you hear that you are an offspring of higher consciousness, there is something within you that responds to and even thrills to it. That something in you is the impersonal I AM that is at the moment being felt personally.

This I AM is that instinct within you, or that place in your consciousness, that has you calling yourself "I" or "me." Until now you have superstitiously thought of yourself as being only a visible physical and mental presence. The personal or objective you, your Walter, has looked at yourself through a tiny peep hole and has only seen a small replica of the infinite impersonal self that you really are. *The two are one – your physical self is the instrument or vehicle through which your impersonal self fulfills its divine purpose.*

At last you are able to see that duality is a myth, because the impersonal self that is manifesting itself as the personal you is universal and omnipresent. In other words, the impersonal divine idea or consciousness that is expressing itself as all individualized beings is also expressing itself personally as your individual self.

Once I understood how my impersonal self was appearing personally as Walter, I no longer had to speculate on whether I existed as a higher consciousness or not. I, the impersonal I within, was experiencing and being itself "as" Walter. I existed as both the observer and the observed.

Every step of our spiritual evolution has prepared us to consciously experience ourselves as I AM. You wouldn't be reading these words if your own consciousness had not drawn this truth into your awareness. When you believe that you lack something that makes it possible for you to recognize who you really are, it means you do not yet fully trust yourself or the impersonal process that is leading you into an awareness of your true being.

To accept the idea that this divine sense of self has always talked to you, look into your past and you will remember that there were experiences and ideas that came to you out-of-the-blue for which you were unable to account. From where did you think those thoughts came? That "blue" they came out of was your impersonal self. Then you will see that all along it was the I AM of you that brought those things into your consciousness from your own unconscious divine mind, from the impersonal "I" within your being.

We have all experienced the law of attraction. When we feel drawn to a teaching or a teacher, it is our impersonal I AM responding to the I AM we sense was or is embodied in that particular teaching or teacher. That is why we are attracted to some teachings and not to others. The more we are consciously or subconsciously aware of our own impersonal I AM, the more we are attracted to those teachings that voice the I AM. A kind of impersonal spiritual chemistry takes place, and that will not happen if the impersonal source is not already active at our personal level. Those occasions are not coincidences. We would not have been drawn to those teachers or writings in the first place if the I of ourselves was not using that as its way of showing us that our I AM is the way, the truth, and the life.

In Greek the word *persona* means "mask." The divine process that is our essential being has given us masks, or personalities, for its own purpose. Up until now we have superstitiously thought that we were our masks, but now we are able to understand that we are divine-humans who are both the masks and the I AM that is wearing the mask.

Your human identity, your personal self or mask, is not a fraud. The I within you has created it for a divine purpose, but the difference now is that through your ability to double-think, your personal self is recognizing the divine impersonal self of your self. You are turning over your human or personal life to the I AM of yourself. In doing so, it also frees you from believing that there is anything outside of yourself upon which you need to depend; you are self-complete. You are like a china cup with an outside and an inside. Each is important to the other; otherwise there wouldn't be a cup.

When you face a difficult situation you can become aware that your impersonal I AM has created the situation in order to tell you something at the personal level. It is your own impersonal self's way of revealing some principle to follow or flaw to be corrected.

The reason the real meaning of I AM had not revealed itself to all but a few in the past is because humankind, in general, had not spiritually matured to the point where it could handle that knowledge until now. The infinite power, intelligence, and influence to which the "I AM" has access could have done great harm before the impersonal self could bring the human ego under its control. It has taken this long for self-centered egotism to be disciplined out of the ego so that it can now be used as the I AM has designed it to be used – as a necessary tool employed to convert idea, consciousness, or perception into visible form.

Our belief in ourselves as the Third Appearance takes place in us when we can double-think and simultaneously be aware of our impersonal I AM self and its expression as our personal selves. Recognizing this I AM awareness constitutes a dramatic shift in both our individual consciousness and in the effect we have on the collective consciousness; therefore, we have to be quick to spot old habits of dualistic thought where we have unintentionally contradicted the omnipotence and omnipresence of the I AM that we are.

Once the gap has been closed between our humanity and our divinity, we will realize and experience the same impersonal I AM source that was in Jesus, Buddha, Einstein, Michelangelo, Shakespeare, and all the other masters of the past. We do not honor those masters or teachers by personalizing them; we honor them by becoming aware that the impersonal I AM, the spirit source that was operating through and as them, is now operating in and as us. The creative source that was in our avatars is the same I AM source that is in us.

Meditation is the time when my intent is to converse with my higher consciousness. When I am successful, it is the time when Walter dialogues with or listens to his I AM self. Because I am grounded in Scriptural language, the words often reflect that background. Here is an example of my listening to my higher self as it talks to Walter:

> *Let go. Let go of your personal sense of self for a moment. In quietness and confidence is your strength. Confide in me, your higher consciousness, which I AM, and I will interpret your life for you. This I that I AM is your impersonal self - your essential being - complete, perfect, and pure. I AM that which gave birth to your human identity. I AM that which has molded you from your first step into the person I have chosen for you to be. I have been with you in all ways, because I AM who you are, or rather you are who I AM as I appear at the visible level.*
>
> *If you make your bed in the hell of human confusion I will be with you, because I AM the impersonal Self, and as such, it is impossible for you to be anywhere without my omnipresence. The only way*

you can have faith in me is to have faith in yourself. Let go of centuries of the false personal sense which said that the you in the world is other than an expression of me, the I AM of you. I AM the air you breathe, the love you love, the life you live. I AM your way, your truth, and your life. Wherever I AM you are. Wherever you are I AM. In quietness and confidence I speak to you for I AM your still small voice. Do unto yourself, as I would have you do unto others, for it is my good pleasure to personalize the kingdom as our life. I am your fullness of joy, your abundance, and your restoration. I AM that within you that comes forth as the love you give to others. And I say this to your divine-human being: 'Well done, good and faithful servant. You are being faithful in all things and now I will make you master of many.' We, the impersonal I AM that is talking to you now and the personal I that is hearing yourself, will always walk together hand-in-hand as one and the same. It is done.

The Impersonal Personal

*I*t is possible for some individuals to have an epiphany when suddenly an intuitive grasp of reality comes through, and a person instantly experiences his or her essential being as the Third Appearance. The rest of us are left to approach the tedious and less dramatic job of examining our old-fashioned, seemingly innocuous, thoughts and feelings one by one in order to eliminate unrecognized roadblocks to our spiritual awakening.

When I arrived at my early fifties it was at though I had a PhD. in higher math and found that I didn't know how to add; something simple was missing. After an intense period of preparatory self-examination, I discovered what it was – I needed to learn instant obedience.

Instant obedience means that the minute a negative, self-depreciative, or spiritually poisonous thought comes into our minds we must *stop it dead in its tracks*. Most of us are "think-a-holics." Once we swallow the first negative thought or unhealthy perception, the second one goes down easier. After that there is another and another until we are psychically drunk or, at the very least, inebriated with self-destroying perceptions. The alternative isn't for us to ignore our problems but to put them aside until our emotions are settled down and under control and we can deal with them on our own terms. Instant obedience changed my life, but it was years later before I realized just how much.

Until I was able to instantly stop my first negative thought, many of my decisions were made by rational judgment based on good and evil, rather than by my innate intuitive spiritual guidance. On those occasions I hadn't used my mind and emotions – they had used me. But once I learned instant obedience, except for a few lapses, I gained control of my mind and didn't automatically respond to instant judgmental impressions. I was able to handle the various crises of perception that life brought to my door with impunity. When a challenge came up, sometimes I had to postpone examining it for a few hours, or even a day or two, until I could get emotions out of the way and Walter centered in his higher consciousness. Eventually I could handle situations with spiritual intent and without self-denial.

After I had learned instant obedience, I had to learn what I now call "impersonalization" in order to *feel* rather than *think* of how to solve my problems and deal with negative judgments.

It sounds contradictory, but it is impossible to personally experience that which is the same in all of us and the universal nature of divinity without being able to impersonalize. Until we can impersonalize God we have a man-made God, a God made in the image and likeness of personal man, and until we can impersonalize others we cannot see the God in them.

I became aware of the subject of personal sense and impersonalization when I read the first edition of *Science and Health*, by Mary Baker Glover, who later became Mary Baker Eddy. It bore little resemblance to later editions of *Science and Health*, as it was less Scriptural and more rhetorical. Its focus was mainly on personal sense and how that could lead us astray. Mrs. Eddy taught that looking at things personally was a misconception of reality. Our dreams seem like reality when we are dreaming them, and she claimed that, in the same fashion, judging life materially and personally is equally fictitious. She stipulated that in order to become free of our misconceptions it is necessary for us to impersonalize our perceptions.

For a good thirty years after I came upon the concept of impersonalization, I wrestled with it unsuccessfully. Finally, I saw the principle involved, and impersonalizing not only became my main *modus operandi* for solving problems; it kept me mentally sober.

Impersonalization is the most important thread in the fabric of spiritual consciousness. What do I mean by impersonalizing, and how do we implement it? There are conditions and responses that are impersonal because they affect everyone. When we are aware of the universal nature of an object, situation, person, or cause, we are able to keep from judging it or referring to it as belonging to any particular person or situation. Bertrand Russell explained, "When I say that a belief is impersonal I mean that those desires that enter into its causation are universal human desires, and not such as are peculiar to the person in question." In defining the impersonal John Dewey wrote, "A machine as compared to a hand tool is an impersonal agency." When we are aware of the universal nature of the stumbling blocks that are in everyone's way, we can understand what is taking place without judging or blaming an individual when we see someone stumble

When we become aware of the universal nature of what we think of as an error without attributing it to a specific person or situation, we can then observe whatever is taking place from the viewpoint of our higher consciousness without poisoning ourselves with personal judgment or personal concern. In other words, we can see that the soul or spiritual being of a person has been hypnotized or masked by his or her looking at things through the lens of personal sense. If we must blame something, we can then blame the condition rather than the person. By experiencing the impersonal nature of a situation, and by releasing the people involved from personal judgment, we can understand the situation and thereby change or heal it.

When Jesus said, "Forgive them for they know not what they do," he was impersonalizing the situation, and instead of blaming those who were crucifying him he attributed their actions to the ignorance that possessed them. We don't have to be Pollyannas, refusing to face our own problems or the ignorance influencing other people's lives, but we can be realistic about those situations and handle them without violating our own spirit of love by judging them objectively.

In order to arrive at a practical solution to our problems and judgments three steps are necessary. We must be realistic about what is taking place at the personal level; we must then impersonalize the situation and negate its influence; and we must find closure by arriving at a present solution that affirms the nature of omnipotence. I had been taught the first two steps a long time ago, but until the spiritual condensate- where the human and the divine are one and the same – became a reality to me, I sensed that something was missing. I had known for a long time how valuable and necessary it was for me to see the impersonal nature of a situation, but without taking it to the third step the sense of duality remained. Something obviously was missing, and when I found out what it was I finally knew how to complete the circle and solve problems while at the same time continuing to love being human.

First, I begin by taking a look at what I am conscious of at any given moment. I look at my personal opinion or my viewpoint toward whatever situation I have been trying to cope with, including its darkside. Carl Jung called that "acknowledging the shadow side of life." I don't ignore the shadows, and I try to look beyond judgment, but as near as possible I face up to what I feel personally on its own terms.

I find that I cannot control how my mind is working and what is taking place within my feelings until I am able to impersonally observe what is going on; however, I must first personally observe the facts before I can impersonally generalize, draw conclusions, and know what to do. Ignoring the personal level as though it does not exist is self-defeating.

Second, after acknowledging my personal feelings and their shadow sides, I consciously stand aside and look at the situation, viewing it impersonally from my higher divine consciousness. If the situation has something to do with me personally, I look at it as though I am watching it happen to someone else. By observing it from that impersonal viewpoint, I can see whether or not I, Walter, have personalized the situation and to what degree I have humanly judged it. When I look at it impersonally I can see whether or not I have been giving the situation power. By removing it from personal judgment and by impersonalizing it, I am then able to neutralize its power.

What do I mean by neutralizing its power? To neutralize is to destroy or render inefficient, to take the power away. Once we become aware that the creative energy we call God, or omnipotence, has been misappropriated and falsely attributed to a situation or person, our experienced understanding neutralizes the problem. All problems give rise to a crisis of perception. When we perceive that there is but one power and one presence in the universe, false appearances are neutralized or nullified and what we have thought of as a spiritual healing takes place.

For years those two steps were enough to transform my life, but when I began to realize that the time had come for me to close the gap between the human and the divine I could see that something else was needed. Unless we add another step, impersonalization alone perpetuates the gap. The third step is for us to *re-personalize*. Personal sense is not the problem; a misinterpretation of the personal level is the problem. If omnipresence and omnipotence are the reality, then after discovering the error in our thinking and neutralizing its power we have to re-personalize and see how God appears in and as what we see personally. Anything less is a rejection of our physical presence.

In other words, after I impersonalize and see the nature of the ignorance that is presently controlling a person, situation, or myself I am able to consciously be aware of how the divine presence is appearing personally. Then after I see "the soul truth" of individuals and circumstances in the light of their divine reality, I complete the circle by re-personalizing or re-seeing the personal, but this time in terms of the divine truth they represent. *That is what love is – the ability to experience the truth of another's being, not despite appearances but because of them.*

We live in a personal world, and it is impossible to fool ourselves into believing that we can ever rise totally above judging the human scene. But, after impersonalizing situations we can then once more double-think and look at the personal level, simultaneously, remembering that the impersonal truth of being exists as our higher consciousness – *the Third Appearance.*

Chapter 6

The Divine Plan

*I*mpersonalization makes it possible for me to disregard the lingering belief that chance plays a part in my life. It demystifies the idea that someone – some God – is keeping score and if I make too many mistakes I will flunk the course. I now see that in all of our lives there is an impersonal divine plan in place, working towards the fulfillment of our spiritual evolution. An awareness of this divine plan is the thread that holds all the others in place.

Hidden within the seed that I plant in my garden is a divine plan for its future. With water and sunshine the seed breaks open and a shoot appears above the surface. In its season flowers appear, and after that the multiplication of new seeds, all part of a divine plan for each individual seed. There is a divine sequence behind the miracle of birth that takes place without conscious intelligence, so there must be a divine plan for my life that I can trust.

As long as we feel personally responsible for our lives we have not turned them over to our higher consciousness, and to some degree our lives remain based on fear. When I became convinced that my life wasn't an accident, but that it had been created and was being fulfilled by a divine plan, fear lost its power over me. We cannot experience ourselves as the presence of God until we realize that no matter what happens to us, there is a divine plan uniquely expressing itself as our individual lives.

Once I became convinced that there is now, and always has been, a self-included divine plan for my individual presence, it was obvious to me that I need not fear temporary setbacks. I may be able to personally slow the plan down, or speed it up, but the outline for my life dictates its fulfillment. I don't believe in predestination as though specific objectives are predetermined, but I do believe the final outcome is. Our individual life-plans may take different forms and have different timing, but by the end we will all awaken to a conscious realization of ourselves as the presence of God.

There are times in my life when the divine plan seems to be temporarily stalled. Perhaps that is because of my own human intervention, a lack of self-love, or even fear. I have learned that when I impersonalize the cause of my setbacks I am able to see how the lessons I need to learn are part of the divine plan. If I remind myself to trust the plan, anxiety turn into self-satisfaction and self-fulfillment. That means that if I don't get the job I think I want, something far better will soon present itself. It means that even if I do the job I want it might be no more than a temporary activity before the plan directed me to something even more rewarding. Sometimes it meant that I had needed to learn something through a specific occupation, and that once I had learned what I needed to learn I was moved on. I found out the hard way that it is wrong for me to try and yank doors open, but it is worse for me not to walk through doors that do open in order to explore what new opportunities the divine plan has to show me.

Our task, yours and mine, is to shed centuries of either-or conditioning – those habitual ways of thinking that keep us believing that we are either our inferior personal selves, who live by law, or that we are our superior impersonal God-selves who live by what we think of as grace. *These two selves are a double-thread, and we must discard anything that keeps us from remembering that we are now all that God is, that the good in our lives is the shining forth of our own essential I AM consciousness. We must add to the fabric of our consciousness the realization that, without a doubt, we trust the divine plan to direct, heal, and fulfill our personal lives.*

The Process

*T*here is a single word that sums up and demystifies the existence of a divine plan, or what it means to live by grace, particularly for those who claim not to believe in such things. It is the word "process." Back in the fifties, when I was producing plays in New York, it was fashionable to reject the word "God" as though it were a dirty word. At that time I was making frequent trips to the Vedanta monastery in California, spending time with the mystic, Joel Goldsmith, and reading everything I could get my hands on about mysticism. In sharing my thoughts and feelings with the group that I ran with, Tennessee Williams, Gore Vidal, Truman Capote, and other Broadway types, I had to come up with another word for "God," so I used the word "process."

Those who consider themselves atheists or agnostics cringe at the thought that their lives revolve around grace or a divine plan. Nevertheless, they are quick to acknowledge that there is a universal process. They will admit that the sun will rise at a specific time tomorrow, that spring will follow winter, and that there is a process at work in all creative acts. They marvel at the process that guides a sperm to fertilize an egg and in the process make some cells form eyes while others form arms and legs. If they didn't trust the process they would be afraid to leave their houses, never drive an automobile, nor cross a busy street. There really are no atheists or agnostics, because acknowledging that there is a working creative process is the equivalent of a belief in God.

If it is difficult for you to put your trust in there being a divine plan for your life, a helpful "how to" is to think of the process that has been ongoing in your life in the past. See if that won't help you realize that there has always been a step-by-step divine evolutionary plan at work guiding you. Both the difficult times and their solutions have been a continuing process with a purpose. If you can muster a conscious trust in the process that has brought you to this point in your life, you can trust it to take you the rest of the way, despite any adverse current appearances.

The one consistent presence that I have felt throughout my life has been the "process" that has been living me. I am not only a temporary physical being, I am the continuous process that has produced and continues to live life as me. That process is what I AM. When I think of the divine process as the I AM, my soul wraps around it.

There is no place I can go where the process that is living Walter does not go, even if I make my bed in hell. The process is the way, the truth, and the life of me. When I meditate on that process, I feel what it means to experience that I AM THAT I AM. I exist, and that existence is the process that I AM.

Let's make it as simple as possible. We can forget all our fancy metaphysics, and can put aside our concepts of God. We can stop thinking of what it means to live by grace. When anxiety rears its head, when challenges appear, when lack or illness show up on the horizon, there is one thing that can take us through anything. We can consciously TTP – *trust the process*.

Synonym Success

*I*n order for me to become aware that my life is a divine process there is another "how to" thread that has helped me connect my early religious conditioning with my present more unconventional understanding. I suggest that when we come across writings of traditional religious language or hear old time-honored prayers, the way to avoid superstition is to use synonyms in place of words that have previously implied a power apart from our own consciousness. When we see or hear the words "God," "Father," or "Lord," if we immediately substitute those words with "my higher consciousness," "love," "the process," or "the divine plan," their substitutions eliminate a sense of duality.

For example, when I hear, "God is closer than breathing, nearer than hands and feet" or that I should "contemplate God's presence within me," it is more meaningful to me if I think, "My Higher consciousness is closer than breathing, nearer than hands and feet," or that I should "contemplate the presence of the divine plan within me."

In similar fashion, when I conptemplate traditional Scripture or prayers, I see them as a present reality rather than wish fulfillment. Most people say the Lord's Prayer in a futuristic sense as though they hope what they ask for will happen, "Our Father, which art in heaven, Hallowed be thy name (in the future). Thy Kingdom come (hopefully). Thy will be done... (in the future)" etc. That's why I find the 23rd Psalm to be more a "now" prayer, as though it is happening at the moment, not that it will be in the future. In doing so, it has been helpful for me to substitute "divine plan" or "the divine process" for "The Lord," and then I do I feel the presence of a divine purpose for my life taking place now.

The divine process is my sheperd, I shall not want. It maketh me to lie down in green pastures. The process leadeth me beside still waters. It restoreth my soul and body. The divine process leadeth me in the paths of righteousness for its namesake. Yea, though I, as a human being, walk through the valley of the shadow of death, I will fear no evil, for the process is fulfilling my life. It is my rod and my staff. The divine process prepareth a table before me in the presence of others. It anointeth my head with truth, my cup runneth over. Surely goodness and mercy will follow me for the rest of the days of my life, and I will live in the consciousness of the divine process for ever.

Horrible Habits

One of the most insidious culprits, and one that tricks us out of living the process spontaneously, is our being enslaved by habits. It is easier to become addicted to habits than to drugs, and the result can be even more devastating as we attempt to live by grace rather than by human judgments. Habits take over our lives and turn us into automatons. They quickly become the laws by which we live, replacing our trust in the process. Habits are the result of laziness. As long as we let them control our daily lives, we stop thinking. If we don't think we, don't listen to our intuition, and intuition is how the spirit talks to us.

Habits are institutionalized thought, and, as such, they are a substitute for security. When we habitually offer ourselves to any kind of organization, mental or physical, we abdicate personal responsibility; we respond to them rather than to the language of spirit. Habits predetermine time and have nothing to do with a life lived in the now. They rob us of freedom, which is our goal in life.

Habits are not exclusively physical actions, and in fact, habitual thought can be even more stifling than physical habits. We have the habit of being governed by our physical bodies, rather than thinking of ourselves primarily as spirit, consciousness, or energy. When habitual concepts become habitual responses, intellect replaces spiritual freedom and adventure, and we are stuck in one boring place. Awareness is the beginning of knowledge; therefore, if we take a good look at the habits to which we have unwittingly become addicted, we are at the entrance to the cathedral of wisdom.

Centuries ago, religious organizations and their leaders realized how important habits were in controlling people. They understood that by encouraging habitual prayers, habitual ceremonies, and habitual attendance, and by dogmatically repeating habitual concepts, their followers would no longer think for themselves.

Routines are helpful to us, but when we become wary of breaking them, we lose sight of ourselves as the presence of God. This became glaringly apparent to me after I developed the habit of meditating a couple of hours every morning. I found that on those days when it was impossible for me to take time to meditate, I felt anxious, almost as though my well-being was dependent on my meditation routine. One day when I had an early appointment and didn't have any time to meditate, I realized how deeply superstition had insinuated itself into my life. I saw that by believing that it was necessary for me to meditate daily, I was denying the omnipotence that I claimed as my heritage. By feeling compelled to meditate, I rejected grace as the *modus operandi* of my life. I now know that if my spirit is in the right place, everything I do is a meditation. I still meditate every morning because I like to, not because it is a habit, and if something intervenes I am not anxious or distressed because I know I can enjoy a time of meditation later on in the day.

Once I stopped being superstitious about missing meditations, I was able to track down and eliminate other habits that had dictated my actions. There are still a number of routines that I follow. I take my vitamins in the morning, I brush my teeth before going to bed, go to the gym twice a week, and I meditate before writing, but I have no fear of missing those routines. I may practice a particular form of prayer for a while, but before very long I change it. I light a candle at meditation time as a symbol of the living spirit, but I'm not superstitious about not doing it when I am away on a trip. I may go to certain gatherings or attend certain programs for a while, and then I remind myself that they are not habitually necessary, or I take a break from them every so often. At times I take a vacation from personal relationships, and I find that on my return I appreciate them more than ever because they are not dulled by habitual routines.

Habits are time-based; they carry the past forward into the now. As I listen to the now of my actions, my security is based on the realization that because I am the presence of the divine, I am no longer being used by anything other than the spirit that I AM.

Continuity and Now

*U*ntil we sense that there is a thread of continuity that connects our essential being to a life beyond this lifetime, we can't consciously experience our divinity. I wasn't able to get a real feel for the divine plan of my life until I no longer thought of my life-span as, at best, four score or more years. Until I stopped thinking logically in terms of time and allowed myself to feel a sense of continuity, which began before and extended after my conscious awareness, my struggle to achieve illumination seemed futile. There wasn't enough time.

Most of us instinctively sense that we didn't just come into being x years ago and that we won't cease to exist in y years to come. Life eternal is not just a metaphysical speculation. Infinity can't be minus anything, so our unique consciousness will always exist in one way or another. Maintaining an awareness of our individual uniqueness and a sense of its continuity is a necessary "how to"; otherwise, as human beings we feel like a yo- yo, up one minute and down the next.

The theory of reincarnation is one of man's attempts to put a face on our sense of continuity. It is an example of trying to explain fourth-dimensional truth in third-dimensional language and thought – something that can't be done. However, accepting the concept of reincarnation is as close as we can come to internalizing what we can't intellectually understand, and it can help us sense the continuity of our spiritual evolution.

Because the most widely accepted theory of reincarnation is based mostly on an objective viewpoint, what it signifies subjectively in terms of consciousness is often overlooked. Rather than believing we have lived as identifiable personalities in another lifetime, we come closer to the truth if we think of ourselves subjectively as having experienced the levels of consciousness symbolized by the those personalities. If we can see ourselves as consciousness with physical bodies rather than physical bodies with consciousness, reincarnation can be understood as a continuity of different levels of our transformative consciousness rather than as different physical reappearances.

The individuation of each soul takes place by going through a number of different stages similar to the different grades that we go through in school. Everyone starts out at a base level and continues up the scale through increasingly advanced levels of consciousness, each one building on the other. In any single lifetime it is unlikely that anyone is consciously aware of all the levels he or she has experienced. However, all of us can to some extent sense a continuity of growth leading up to where we are currently. In doing so, we recognize the eternality of our existence – that our essential being will continue after we discard our present bodies. We can say, as Jesus did, "Before Abraham was, I AM."

There are more people alive on earth today than all those who have lived in the past combined. In terms of levels of consciousness, how does that help us to understand today's world? It does it in two ways. First, it means that there are many "new" people who are at the beginning levels of consciousness, and that they are approaching life from whatever stage of evolution they are now at. Second, it helps us to realize that every level of consciousness is simultaneously represented somewhere on earth, and it would be a mistake for us to expect everyone to approach life in the same way as we do.

Our natural tendency is to think that everyone has the same feelings as we do, and that they will respond in the same way we would under similar circumstances. Despite the fact that we are all *Homo Sapiens*, the different levels of consciousness that motivate people who have been conditioned in dissimilar cultures and backgrounds makes us the equivalent of a number of different species.

Once we understand that because we are at different stages of the consciousness-evolution it is impossible for all of us to think the same way, to respond emotionally with the same intensity, or to embrace the same values, it helps us to find ways of communicating with the differences in others.

Having a sense of continuity is essential, as long as we can keep it from getting in the way of being fully present in the moment. When we try to equate what it means to live in the now in terms of time, past or future, we are literally living in borrowed time. When I realized that to live in the now means to no longer react to my past or future impulses, I could feel an unconditioned response to now. When I reacted to thoughts whose roots were in a past action or if I anticipated a future feeling, I was reacting rather than acting.

Without losing a sense of life's continuity, I began to appreciate what it means to live in the now once I realized that it is impossible to worry or fear without projecting myself out of the present moment. Fears are the future, while worries are past reactions intruding on now. For example, at this very moment you are reading this book and are not thinking in terms of having any other needs, but the minute you start to fear or worry you are indulging in a past regret or a future desire and have projected yourself out of the now. We can't make the future be now, no matter how hard we try. Once the future arrives the current now no longer exists.

My Family

There is still another thread needed to complete our fabric of consciousness, to weave together our divine plan, the process, and continuity. It is the sense of what constitutes our spiritual family. In the past I said that I was one with the family of all humankind, but when I said it I was only thinking in terms of the physical side of life and the material limitations we all share. Obviously, my body is not one with other bodies, so who or what is the "me" that is one with others? In order to understand, I had to arrive at a fourth-dimensional answer where time and space are not factors. Since I am consciousness I could say that I am one with the collective consciousness and, therefore, I share the interests of all human beings, but that is not quite accurate. I feel that I am really only one with those who are of my spiritual family, my household. What do I mean by household?

In metaphysical symbolism "house" stands for consciousness. When Jesus said, "In my Father's house are many mansions," he was saying that in his higher consciousness were many different expressions of his spirit. Objectively, families share a bloodline. Subjectively, our spiritual households, or families, are those who share the same level of consciousness and values that we do.

When Jesus was told that his mother and his brethren were outside he replied, "Who is my mother and who are my brethren?... For whosoever shalldo the will of my Father which is in heaven, the same is my brother, and sister, and mother." In other words, he believed his family – his household – was not defined by shared blood but by shared consciousness. It is the same today. Our spiritual families are those who have arrived at the same level of consciousness that we have. Sometimes we must choose the family to which we prefer to show allegiance from either those who primarily believe in an objective material approach or those who live primarily from subjective spiritual values.

Time and space are not factors in consciousness. Although Jesus left the human scene two-thousand-years-ago, in those moments when we experience the anointed or subjective level of consciousness that he attained, we are one with him. His family is our family, his household our household. Through the evolution of individual spiritual consciousness, the spiritual family continues to grow, and there are now more of us capable of experiencing the anointed level of consciousness than ever before.Because I am connected to the collective consciousness, how I handle what troubles me to some degree affects the collective consciousness itself, particularly those of my consciousness-family. This is true even though I do not know each of them personally. When I work through difficult situations and become more enlightened, I am not just doing it for myself; I am adding to the collective self.

The most important thing for me to do at those times when I sense an undefined anxiety and feel cut off from the family is to release it by going into meditation in order to heal myself as best I can. I try to remember all that I know of a spiritual nature to eliminate dualistic thinking and to reconnect with my spiritual household and my divine-human self.

There are times when I am more successful than others, but I have learned that when I feel a psychic pressure for which there is no obvious personal cause, it is better for me to avoid trying to figure out where I personally went astray. It is likely that I have tuned into a disturbance that is affecting the collective consciousness in areas that are important to me and to my consciousness-family.

When something affects a state of consciousness to which my family and I relate, a change takes place in my spiritual chemistry and I feel it. For instance, I have found that when world leaders are attempting to initiate controls or negative policies in areas that are spiritually important to me, I sense it. That's because the spiritual consciousness they are detrimentally affecting is my consciousness – is me. In the same way, those of your consciousness are your collective family, no matter where they are in the world or what religion they practice. When things are being done that are not in accord with your shared spirit, you and all those of your spiritual household personally feel it. There are also days when I feel an unidentifiable joy or bliss, and that is most likely because the truths that I value are succeeding somewhere in the world of my spiritual family.

The good news in all of this is that we are not alone. We can feel the presence of our spiritual family at any time, and can turn to it in times of need. We are a joined circle of spiritual beings tied together in a belief system that reflects our collective consciousness. What affects one of us affects all of us. That is how we are "one in spirit" with our fellow beings, in sharing consciousness we are one with each other.

We also know that although we may still see ourselves as finite beings, we are not. As individuals we do have a finite shape and size, just like that wave in the ocean. We may start from the standpoint of our finite selves, but when we go within and experience the infinity of our selves, we are a part of the collective consciousness that can and does affect the world. Through our collective spiritual family we can individually counter the influences that are trying to negate spiritual power or fourth-dimensional consciousness. We do that by experiencing who we are in the new role we play in the human-spiritual drama. We reinvent ourselves in the image of our divine humanity where we are both the ocean and the wave.

Involution and Evolution

*F*or us to conceive of a self that is continuous, active, and eternal, our verb self rather than our noun self, we have to see our human lives not only in terms of an ebb and flow but also as a spiral. Until we finally reach the spiritual condensate level of consciousness we are not only products of evolution but also of involution. For example, an atom becomes a part of a body, but when the body dies and disintegrates the atom separates itself and returns to the source. It becomes part of another body, perhaps a flower or a rock this time. Involution is that process of returning to the source, to essential cause. Every thing that exists in form undergoes both evolution and involution. We like to think of evolution because it promises improvement, but we disdain involution because it looks like a step backwards.

Involution not only refers to what is taking place within, but it is what it means to be involved. If you are involved with something you are a part of that something. Life is a constant spiral of involution and evolution. Perhaps when we experience ourselves as Third Appearance consciousness, involution and evolution will be recognized as one process, but until then we can better understand, if we have an awareness of how they affect our daily human lives.

Today even medical science admits that our transient substance is not our essential being. All the cells or atoms that make up our tiny bodies as babies soon leave, and new ones form a more mature body. That proves that our essential being is not material – we are not atoms, but the consciousness that creates, assembles, and disassembles the atoms. We are the process of involution and evolution by which our higher consciousness our God-self, grows our bodies and will one day cause them to disintegrate. We are the circle of life involving and evolving. That which is continuing on is our soul, our eternal nature which was never born and which will never die. The body was born and will die, but the soul was never born because it never was material. This realization is how the principle of spiritual healing is substantiated, freeing us from conceiving of ourselves as embodying disease and limitation.

Stephen Hawkin's big bang theory is a dramatic example of how modern-day scientists are explaining involution and evolution, but it is far from being a new concept. In a lecture given in 1896, Swami Vivekananda explained it and even anticipated Einstein's theory of the involution and evolution of time and space. He said that though life seems like a straight line, eventually that line curves and becomes a circle, a matter of involution and evolution. Einstein didn't discover that truth; he just dipped into the source and gave us the mathematical formula for it.

Often in oriental religions it is taught that the essential self is omnipresent since its being is what we now identify as consciousness and it's not limited by time, space, or form. That would imply that I am you, and you are me, because we are each expressions of universal consciousness. At death we do not lose our individuality. My unique being, though a manifestation of the one, all-inclusive, omnipresent soul, still retains its uniqueness. My soul and your soul are the same One soul, but at the same time each of our souls is infinite and remains infinitely individual. You and I are a point in that one soul, a microcosm of the macrocosmic soul. Though individuals, we are all that soul is.

The uniqueness of each individual soul could not be accepted until now without limiting the soul, because the capacity to double-think, when the process of involution and evolution are seen as one process, had not evolved.

Ordinary Spirituality

As we become aware of the presence of our own higher consciousness and how it translates into our daily lives, we feel less and less dependent on outside influences such as churches, organizations, or teachers when they claim they have something exceptional for us. As long as our spiritual lives are considered to be extraordinary, the gap between our divinity and our humanity still exists and we have yet to realize our potential as the presence of God – the Third Appearance.

The dictionary defines "ordinary" as "customary, usual, and normal." Everything we customarily do or say is representative of some quality of spirit. It can be a negative spirit or a positive one, but either way the spirit we express in everything we do or say is what creates our lives for better or for worse. Until we are ordinarily aware of the spirit of love, we still have further to go.

In order to be aware of how ordinary spirit is, we need to create a new language. We need a language that reflects the kind of spirit inherent in what we say, rather than having only intellectual content. Everything we say and every act we perform carries a spiritual message that is more important than the actual words we speak. We are verbs, and verbs always project a quality of spirit, whether positive or negative. We are not a spiritual being at one moment and not another. Until we become diligently and constantly conscious of what spirit we are projecting, we will not send out a clear picture of our essential being. Spirit is subjective matter, and although as human beings we can't be spiritual, we *can* express spirituality. We express the spirit of that which we perceive, and that becomes what we create for, in, and as ourselves.

Once being spiritual is seen as ordinary it will no longer be an issue, how we consciously express it will be the issue. In that respect, the state of mind we consider to be "praying without ceasing" will take on a new meaning; we will be monitoring the spirit in our words and actions without ceasing.

Under the guise of creating a better world, religions perpetuate the very belief that keeps us from being what they claim we should be. Some religions keep themselves in business by selling their followers the idea that being spiritual is a moral issue, that it is other than ordinary and natural. When living by the spirit of love becomes an everyday, normal part of our lives, there won't be any more religions – we won't need them. Once we solve the crisis of perception and consciously realize how our spirit works through our perceptions, we will know how to alter them so that they reflect the love that is who we are.

If, as quantum physics claims, everything that we see is consciousness (or spirit) projected as form, then when we stop judging human nature as something that needs to be eliminated, it will cease being a false projection of who we are. Once that happens, we will realize that all we have thought heaven to be is already present on earth. We have missed seeing it in the past because the best way to hide a secret is to put it in plain sight where it appears obvious and ordinary.

Being spiritual is normal and necessary. We don't think that eating breakfast is special because we ordinarily do it. We don't think that sleeping is anything out of the ordinary because we normally do it. Such things are ordinary because we cannot live without them, and it is the same with spirit. Once we routinely monitor the language of spirit that we express in our words and actions, we will realize that those things we have previously thought of as miracles – things like spiritual healing or giving birth – are actually very ordinary.

At the spiritual condensate level we won't think of ourselves as having one identity or another, where the natural man and the spiritual man are in opposition. When that happens we will see how Paul led us astray by saying, "The natural man receiveth not the things of the spirit of God: for they are foolishness unto him: neither can he know them, because they are spiritually discerned." In reverse, the spiritual man cannot know the natural man because he appears objectively and spirit is subjective. The natural man may be unable to understand spirit because it is a different dimension, but without that dilemma we wouldn't be pushed into learning the lessons that eventually make us conscious beings. The natural and the spiritual are just two different dimensions of the one self and when both are lived perfectly in terms of their own levels then they will be the equivalent of each other. Once we no longer see our identities as being in competition, we will realize that it is natural and ordinary to be divine.

To make our spirituality a natural part of our lives we must demystify the symbols we usually associate with spirituality, such as the religious costumes we wear, the emblems that hang around our necks, and the Bibles we hold in our hands. As long we attribute special powers to material symbols, we create a barrier between what we think of as spiritual and the ordinary trappings of life. Anything that isn't seen as ordinary supports the dual belief that God and we are not the same, that spirit is superior to nature.

The Bible was put together by ordinary men and women who were sometimes inspired and sometimes not. Of itself, it has no mystical power. You can throw it on the floor or burn it in a fire and nothing will happen to you because there is no magical power in the ink and paper, nor even in the words written on its pages. Nevertheless, when the truths that are in the *Bible* are internalized and experienced they do have an effect because of what happens to the consciousness of the one who is reading it, but not because of the physical Bible itself. The mystery is self-created by the one using the Bible as a spiritual textbook.

Churches and holy shrines were built by ordinary men out of ordinary materials because of a natural desire to experience the presence of God. As buildings they have no extraordinary power. We can look to them for inspiration, but what we feel is a self-created, self-inspired experience that comes to us not because of but despite of the bricks and mortar. We deny omnipresence when we believe that special places have more of God in them than others. The value of making pilgrimages to special places is in the spirit of one's dedication, not the place itself.

The downside of seeing the world and everything in it as ordinary is that unless we are also aware of the divine in everything we are in danger of losing the magic. We live in the world of common appearances that can be transformed in seemingly magical ways when our higher consciousness is experienced. If you consider those individuals, whom you believe to be masters, or spiritually advanced human beings whose lives appear to be magical, you will find that they seldom get angry, fearful, upset, or judgmental. That is because those emotions come from believing that what happens in life is not ordinary, not customary, usual, or normal. An illumined being is one who sees God in ordinary circumstances and ordinary people.

Self-Fulfilling Prophecy

It is quite true that we must ordinarily see God-consciousness as the one power and one presence, but not for the reasons most people believe. God is an energy that can't do anything unless it is activated by consciousness; therefore, whatever it is within each of us individually that activates consciousness is actually the power. That something is the power of our self-fulfilling prophecies.

The single most important "how to," the one that literally dictates the conditions of our human lives and gives us control over circumstances, involves understanding and being conscious of the significance of self-fulfilling prophecies. Spiritually we are already all that God is, our divine consciousness is the life, the mind, and the spirit of our individual being, but until we realize how to bring those qualities into being they might as well not exist. That method, or "how to," is our use of self-fulfilling prophecy.

Once I discovered how my perceptions created self-fulfilling prophecies, there was no way I could continue to look for a scapegoat or a God that I could blame for my shortcomings or disappointments. After I had swallowed all the metaphysical aspirins I could take, I had to finally acknowledge that my entire life has been the result of my own self-fulfilling prophecies. The perceptions I energized became the self-fulfilling prophecies that manifested themselves in my life for better or worse. The Gospel of John claims the same, "In the beginning was the word [the prophecy] … and the word was made flesh and dwelt among us."

From the time we wake up in the morning until we put our heads on our pillows at night, absolutely everything we encounter is a direct result of what we anticipate or imagine. Even such ordinary activities as eating breakfast or changing clothes are the result of self-fulfilling prophecies. When people have trouble going to sleep at night it may be because they prophesied that they would have trouble going to sleep. Their prophecy fulfilled itself and kept them awake. Our simplest actions are carried out as a result of our prophecies.

Though I didn't know what it really meant when I first read in Isaiah "I will go before thee, and make the crooked places straight," a kind of warm, fuzzy superstition fanned my imagination. It was comforting and hopeful to believe that because I was on the side of the angels my personal difficulties would be made easier. However, once I realized that there was no God taking care of me outside of my own higher consciousness, superstition began to wear thin. I was forced to ask myself what could possibly go before me to make my life's crooked places straighten out? The answer was self-fulfilling prophecy.

Similar to delayed re-play on television, our prophecies precede the forms that eventually appear in our lives. If our perceptions are spiritually healthy, creative, positive, and loving, they keep crooked places from showing up in our lives. In other words, what's in our consciousness goes before us to help us avoid the crooked places. Once we have become aware of the Godly power of our own perceptions and how through self-fulfilling prophecy they create the crises we face today, the effect on our own lives and the future of the world are under our control.

Our lives are entirely created by the perceptions we translate into self-fulfilling prophecies; therefore, we are not helpless victims of any outside influences. Some prophecies we have invented at the moment and some were handed down to us by society. Some we have unwittingly created by watching the news and commercials on television, and others were previously coded into our subconscious by past experiences. To the degree that we have accepted the theological claim that all human beings are sinners, we have self-fulfilled that prophecy as well.

It is human nature to want to blame someone, something, or perhaps the conditions we were born into for the difficulties we encounter, but science has now pulled the rug out from under that form of escapist excuse by proving that as we mature everything in our lives is created by our perceptions manifesting as self-fulfilling prophecies.

Through the power of our imagination we activate or empower consciousness, which, in turn, becomes self-fulfilling prophecy. When we combine an understanding of the deceptive nature of contradiction with the realization of how through our perceptions we create our reality, we will observe to what extent our lives have materialized as the product of those prophecies. It is then that we can change our lives by monitoring our perceptions. As I said earlier, whereas in the past it was a virtue to be positive and think loving thoughts, now we know that it is an undeniable necessity if we want to create happy successful lives for ourselves. No one else can do it for us.

Though I didn't know the principle of self-fulfilling prophecy until years later, I can now see how my fertile imagination created a success scenario that became factual in my early life. At the end of World War II I went straight to New York, and with very limited past experience I had immediate and extraordinary success. In the first year as an actor I played the juvenile lead in three Broadway plays, followed by leading roles on Studio One and Philco Playhouse on television. I became more and more interested in the production aspect of theater, and a few years later I became the youngest producer at that time to win the New York Drama Critics best play award for producing the play, *I Am A Camera*, which was later made into the musical *Cabaret*. Years later I realized that my success wasn't because I had an egotistical assumption that I could do it, but rather it was because I didn't see of any reason why I couldn't do it. I positively prophesied the possibility, and by doing so I created the reality.

Ignorance tricks us into believing that we are affected by the local, national, and international traditions and conditions that surround us, but in fact when they affect us, it is not that they in themselves have any power. At some time in the past we have been indoctrinated with the commonly accepted belief that those conditions do affect us, and, in perceiving that to be true, we ourselves empower them for ourselves. Because we have agreed with the collective ignorance, we have individually allowed our own imaginations to energize and turn that ignorance into self-fulfilling prophecies.

I'm talking about ideas like the common belief that you cannot succeed without knowing the right people, that at such and such an age you will need to wear glasses, that at another period in your life you will no longer be able to make love, that babies have to be born through pain, or that your security depends upon accumulating a large bank account. Unless those mentally assumed laws are consciously negated, we subconsciously manifest them through self-fulfilling prophecy.

When I finally realized that nothing affected my life apart from my own God-given consciousness operating as my self-fulfilling prophecies, it was a hard pill for me to swallow. It left me no place to hide and no one to blame – not a church, not my family, not a partner, not a nation.

It would be simple if self-fulfilling prophecy were always a conscious activity, but what we have to factor in is the enormous importance of our subconscious mind. We all remember times when we were sure everything was going to be just as we wanted, but things didn't turn out that way. What we hadn't counted on were the preconditioned doubts that existed at a subconscious level, waiting to be activated as self-fulfilling prophecies at a later time. However, the subconscious is conditioned by conscious thinking; therefore, if we open ourselves to our higher consciousness we can override past conditioning and revise unintentional negative responses.

There is the familiar Biblical quote, *Psalm 91*, that says, "A thousand shall fall at thy side and ten thousand at thy right hand; but it shall not come nigh thee." In other words, in the dwelling place of those who live in the secret place of the most high. What it is really saying is that those who are tuned into their higher consciousness, to the Third Appearance, will not empower a self-fulfilling prophecy of death and destruction even though they may be surrounded by destructive possibilities.

What we commonly call faith is also an example of the principle of self-fulfilling prophecy. If through our faith we fully and completely accept the belief that the results we desire will take place, we set forth a self-fulfilling energy that creates the very things we have faith in. There is nothing superstitious or religious about it; we do it ourselves. That is why Jesus said, "Whatsoever ye ask in prayer, *believing*, ye shall receive." God doesn't do it for you. Your experienced belief becomes a self-fulfilling prophecy.

Not long ago I heard a woman on public radio say that she had a terminal illness, but that she had prayed to Jesus and Jesus healed her. At first I was skeptical, until I realized that her belief that Jesus could heal her *is what healed her*. She healed herself through her self-fulfilling prophecy. Believing is the key; thinking doesn't do it. If you lift your belief into the experiential level, where you perceive your belief as a reality, it will become a self-fulfilled prophecy.

Remember the story of the man who prayed that the mountain outside his window be moved? The next morning when he looked out his window it was still there, and he said, "I thought so," meaning that he never really believed it was possible for the mountain to move, so it didn't. His disbelief became his self-fulfilled prophecy.

If you believe without a doubt that there aren't any powers working in your life apart from your own higher consciousness, it will become a self-fulfilling fact. If doubt remains, to that degree the doubt will be what you empower. We are the God that is the only power operating in our lives, and that power operates out of our self-fulfilling prophecies.

Purpose

What I am going to discuss now is not a "how to," but rather a "must have" thread in our lives. One rainy morning on my ranch in Texas someone had left the gate open to the lawn and garden area around the main buildings, and several horses were having a high old time eating the flowers. Much to my displeasure, I had to go into the rain to chase them out. Just as I came back inside, I got a telephone call from an old friend telling me that one of our old writer's circle, a very talented and highly successful author, had committed suicide. My first reaction was to be furious, until I thought more about it and understood what had happened. Though my author-friend had plenty of money, good health, and considerable acclaim, he had stopped writing and had lost his motivation. He had lost his purpose in life, and having purpose is what makes life worth living. I sat down and thought for a while about the purpose for my own life, and when I did I became grateful for the rain and the horses. Among other purposes for my life, they gave me a reason to live. I had to chase the horses out!

It is of the greatest importance for each of us to recognize our purpose for our being alive at this time and decide whether or not we are about our main purpose, even if our purpose seems menial and insignificant in terms of the dramatic things that are taking place in the world. Close your eyes for a moment and ask yourself if you have a purpose of life. As yourself what is it? Are you fulfilling it?

All human beings have the same underlying purpose – to push forward the evolution of life on earth. As human beings we represent different stages of evolution leading toward our ultimate purpose. A child just learning the alphabet isn't at the point of reading Shakespeare, though in time he or she may be.

It is necessary for you to realize that every stage you go through represents a step forward in the evolution of your consciousness. When you are fully conscious, you will perceive yourself as one with and as the presence of God. That is the purpose of your being here.

What does it mean to be fully conscious? It means for you to attain what Paul called "having that mind that was in Christ Jesus." I believe that Jesus, in the West, and Buddha, in the East, represented that moment in the advancement of human evolution when the first fully-conscious humans began to evolve. They were fully conscious of the spiritual nature of all life, conscious of the unity of all that exists, and conscious of the all-inclusive nature of omnipresence that dispelled the illusion of duality.

Pierre Teilhard de Chardin, a trail-blazing paleontologist priest wrote, "All action is complemented by thought, purpose, and desire. It is up to us to be aware of that energy, know how to release it through our faith in its divine purpose, and understand that through our consciousness we are co-creators with that energy."

The divine purpose for all human existence is for us, individually and collectively, to mature to the place where we are not only fully conscious, but where we realize we are consciousness itself. Then we can evaluate every experience in this context and see how it fits into the divine plan. Every experience, good or bad, is present in our lives for one purpose: to make us conscious beings. We can waste the lessons that accompany our experiences and have to go through them over and over again, or we can listen to what they are telling us and become conscious beings. Once we reach the spiritual condensate level of consciousness we will fulfill our purpose for being born, we will realize that we are consciousness itself.

Chapter 7

The Guilt Game

The word "guilt" comes from an old English word meaning "to find fault." Whenever we find any fault with ourselves, or personalize a mistake we may have made, we are feeling guilty.

If we allow ourselves to feel guilty at any time for any reason, we immediately separate ourselves from the realization of our essential being, and we find ourselves embracing superstition. That doesn't mean that in the process of our growth, we do not make mistakes. Mistakes are how we learn, but there is no excuse for letting our mistakes cause us to swallow the poison of guilt. If there is a devil (a metaphor or symbol for self-defeating ignorance), it is guilt.

Subconsciously, a long time ago, I knew that guilt was my enemy. Though I wasn't quick to judge, the one thing that always made me angry was when someone tried to or succeeded in making me feel guilty. I didn't know then that my anger was a reaction to being seen as other than a spiritual being. My refusal to accept guilt was a spiritual defense mechanism.

Whether guilt is an unfortunate aftermath resulting from unachieved goals, or the mechanism by which both religious and educational institutions control their constituents, it is time for us to become aware of its side-effects and resist it with our whole being. Teachings that encourage us to feel guilty for imperfectly following their tenets choke the spirit out of us. *The true purpose of spiritual teaching is not to tell us who we aren't, but to show us who we are – the presence of God.*

Once we get over the belief that by going to one more class or by reading one more book we will find some final answer that will make us better people than we already are, guilt then loses one of its major means of perpetuating itself. We are already perfect human-divine beings in the process of growing into a conscious awareness of our essential being. We can now see that all those things that we thought were our shortcomings were actually blessings, because having to deal with them spurred our growth process.

The confusions we have about who we are often arise because we try to compare what we are going through with the "whats" and "hows" of the past. In doing so, we are in danger of immobilizing ourselves by looking back, just as Lot's wife did. However, we can avoid guilt and spiritual stagnation if we can overcome the either-or syndrome by seeing how the valuable aspects of the old, exclusive, teacher-driven approach can be combined with the more subjective and inclusive spirit-guided way of doing things.

Individually, when we are free of self-doubt it means that we can continue to learn without feeling subservient to others or feeling guilty. For us to learn without subservience, we have to stop being obedient to anything other than our impersonal I AM, the higher consciousness that is within or as us. Once we realize that we cannot learn anything that is not already in our own consciousness, we can appreciate and enjoy studying with others who share our truths.

The underlying and unrecognized cause that gave rise to the concept of original sin is that as human beings we are born with limited capacities, yet we instinctively realize that because we are made in the image of God it is our nature to be infinite. As such, we at times have a sense of guilt for not expressing our infinity.

Even the teachings that embody the I AM as a mystical possibility blindside the experience by making it something that can only happen in the future. By implying that we will be spiritual when we have transcended personal sense, they tempt us to feel guilty for being personal. If we can remind ourselves that the personal is how the impersonal appears at the personal level, guilt loses a major way of tricking us.

One of the main tenets of metaphysical churches is to free individuals from the concept of personal sin and guilt by claiming those are aspects of a universal ignorance that they have temporarily accepted. Sometimes they then inadvertently make us feel guilty by asking in a patronizing tone of voice, "What were you thinking that made that happen?" By implying that we had done something wrong, they prove that they are not thinking of us as our divine impersonal selves, but rather only as limited human beings. They are not acknowledging that our personal selves were created by, and are aspects of, the impersonal. *All else is duality.*

At the impersonal level of our essential being there are no mistakes. That is because our so-called mistakes are a part of the process which creates whatever we are experiencing as part of the divine plan. Mistakes mold the personal self, so there is no need to feel guilty about making them. There is no way we can impersonally judge what is happening to us. At the personal level, the impersonal is appearing problematically as right or wrong. At the impersonal level, a divine purpose is at work and there is nothing to feel guilty about.

Once we become aware that we are facing an extra-ordinary universal transition taking place in the world, in the collective consciousness, we no longer feel personally responsible for finding all the answers, either for ourselves or for the world. We can turn it over to the impersonal I AM that is our individual being. Then we can love ourselves enough to know that "...he which hath begun a good work in you will perform it ..."

To put an end to the last of the superstitions that keep us from recognizing that we are the Third Appearance, we must examine ourselves to see that there isn't a tinge of guilt or fear in us. If we feel that we are falling short then something is wrong; perhaps not with us, but with the teaching or teacher we have tried to follow.

The Student-Teacher Paradox

*T*eachers as well as teachings can be efficient guilt-machines. On the one hand they can help us grow, but on the other hand they can make us feel inferior and guilty. If we cannot practice what they teach as perfectly as they tell us to, or if we believe they have knowledge that we are not heir to, then guilt hides behind the truths those teachings offer.

All teachings are potentially serpent's apples, mine included. By their very nature they imply that if we will embody their advice we will become superior to the person we presently are. If they strive to make us think that at some future time or "knowing" we will be better than we are now, that perception is the very thing that will keep us from realizing that we are already there.

Let's look at teachers for a moment. A teacher's goal should be to impart what knowledge he has and then let his students go. If the students don't leave on their own, they should be kicked out. A successful teacher constantly puts himself out of work, while others keep their students dependent on them so that they can accumulate a large following and abundant support. I have found that most spiritually motivated teachers do not have extremely large followings. If you look closely you will see that many ministers who pack mammoth churches each Sunday, or those who have TV programs watched by multitudes, create a dependency by telling their people what to think and how to live their lives. When followers are asked to subordinate themselves to systems of discipline, they sacrifice freedom on the altar of dependency.

As a general rule, most human beings want someone else to think for them. They want to be told what to do so that they do not have to take personal responsibility for their lives, they do not really want to be free. They do not trust themselves, nor do they trust their divine plans to show them the way to live. They do not realize that being willing to think for themselves and make mistakes results in personal growth.

We study religions and philosophies to become free of any kind of limitation, and yet we are afraid of really being free. It is a paradox that demands too much self-love. Our fear of total freedom signals a lack of a true understanding of who we are, and until we recognize and honor our essential being, self-love escapes us. However, as long as we continue to think of ourselves in egotistical terms, as the bodies we see in our mirrors , it is right for us to be afraid of freedom. If we are to be present as the Third Appearance, we have to be able to associate with, but be completely free of dependence on external attachments, such as teachers or their teachings.

Earlier I mentioned that among a number of teachers I've learned from, the two teachers that were most significant in my life were Joel Goldsmith and Swami Pravananda. When I first met them, I was so in awe of them and the truths that I heard from them that I said few words in their presence. That student-teacher intimidation lessened somewhat over the years, yet I lived in fear of losing their approval.

After fifteen years of intense study at Goldsmith's side, it was as though a switch was suddenly thrown and we no longer communicated. He might as well have been speaking Greek and me Chinese. The break culminated in a nearly complete disconnect, and for a couple of painful years I was confused as to why it had happened. His rejection finally brought me to the point where I was forced to turn inward to that which I found solely within myself. As a result I finally felt all right about letting him go.

Later I realized that what Goldsmith had given me was the greatest gift a teacher can give a student; he had set me free. It wasn't as though he had psychologically figured out that it was time to kick me out of the nest so that I would stand on my own spiritual feet; he was simply following his instinctive inner guidance. After I became used to my spiritual independence, Goldsmith and I had a wonderful reunion. Then we were no longer teacher and student but instead had a relationship of equal sharing, a true oneness for which I am eternally grateful.

Though our student-teacher relationships are necessary and important, when we personalize them they are often misunderstood and can result in our feeling that we are inferior to the teacher or that we lack something within ourselves. We also find statements in the teachings we have studied that were true for us at one time, but that are no longer applicable to who we are today. That may not be a failure of the teaching, but proof of its success. A true teaching's purpose is to prepare us to go beyond where it left off. If we have not eventually gone beyond where our great teachers left us, Jesus included, then those teachers were failures. When Jesus said, "greater works than these shall ye do," he likely meant that we would eventually reach greater levels of expanded consciousness.

I was finally able to appreciate myself and not feel inferior to anyone when I realized that as a person Jesus, just like Walter, wasn't always right. As I have often said, Jesus was perfect but not flawless. He was a perfect example of what it means to be an evolving, growing, divine-human. He was perfect precisely because he had human fallibilities to contend with, and he triumphed over them just as we can. It is important for us to know that though at times he made what could be considered mistakes, Jesus' choices weren't mistakes in the long run any more than yours and mine are. His impersonal God-self led him through the lessons he needed to learn so that he could evolve into the risen Christ, just as your and my impersonal selves are doing the same for us. If Jesus hadn't had flaws to contend with, we couldn't identify with him. By seeing his human side we can now see that even with all our flaws, we too are divine-humans who are also on our way to ascension consciousness.

Often when I have been on a lecture tour, I have had people come up to me and tell me that they believe I have gone beyond my teachers. At first that bothered me because I knew that I had not yet fully integrated some of their profound revelations. But then I finally understood the explanation that allows me to appreciate what my teachers have given me and yet be true to myself without feeling inferior. Subjectively I have not gone beyond my teacher's teachings, but objectively I have expanded or extended them and perhaps eliminated a few of their contradictions.

In truth, we never really have any teacher other than the one that exists inside ourselves. When we hear or read something that we respond to and accept, we do so because our inner teacher is in agreement. It is our own inner teacher who draws us to speakers, writers, and teachers as its way of teaching us. It is important to remember that nothing affects us that is not of our own doing. The truths of which we may have just become aware have been right in front of us all of our lives. It is just that at this particular time we have come to the point in our spiritual evolution where our inner teacher has helped us to open up to greater depths.

Because you are advancing and continuing to grow, you will eventually find flaws in teachings or teachers that you once accepted without question. The paradox is that even then the true teacher-student relationship is working, because when a teacher or teaching leads you to a point where you become aware of their flaws, in that way the flawed teachings are continuing to teach you.

If you feel that it is unworthy of you to make corrections to the teachings you have encountered, that is because you are still accepting the myth of infallibility. Eventually we must stop looking at our teachers, priests, and ministers as superior beings that we need to emulate, and simply appreciate them for what they are. They are avenues of consciousness, and their knowledge is not their personal possession so much as an expression of universal consciousness. We can appreciate their good qualities, but when we personalize them we are in danger of forgetting our equally divine presence.

I am deeply appreciative of those teachers who have been the avenues through which I have received illumination, and I honor them as beloved vehicles through which my awakening has come. However, by the nature of infinitely expanding truth, I have yet to find a single human being, dead or alive, who has arrived at the final truth or who does not at times contradict his or her own teaching. To believe that truth is a personal possession of any individual can leave you with an aftertaste of self-perceived spiritual poverty.

Intimidating people in order to maintain control has long been a conscious procedure, whether implemented by leaders of governments or of religions. Great temples or cathedrals have been built more for the purpose of intimidating people and encouraging them to accept the authority of the establishment than to honor God.

Though spiritual leaders may clothe themselves in fancy robes and wear gold symbols to celebrate a spiritual ritual, the vestments they wear tend to separate them from their followers and imply a spiritual superiority. In turn that causes their followers to feel spiritually inferior, and that feeling of inferiority can become a self-fulfilling prophecy.

As long as we believe that ancient teachings were infallible and that they had some perfect knowledge that we now have to rediscover, we are fooling ourselves. If there had been any complete or perfect teaching in the past, the world would not be in its present condition nor at its present level of consciousness.

Anything that keeps us from perceiving that we are now all that God is keeps us from closing the gap between our divinity and our humanity. We capitalize the word "God" for the same reason that we capitalize the word "I." God and I are the same, and anything that causes us to think otherwise shows that we have not graduated to an awareness of our essential being, the I AM.

If we must be beholden to something, let it be to the process. All religions and philosophies encompass some of the same truths, but none include all the truth. To believe otherwise is to deny the infinity of one's own being.

I am not suggesting that you should immediately reject all teachers, teachings, or religions, but I am saying that the secret of taking dominion, of being fully in possession of your own life, is achieved when you can use everything and not be used by anything. As long as you believe that only one religion has the answer or that only one teacher can help you, you are used by that religion or teacher. When you are grateful for what you are receiving but not dependent on anyone or anything other than your own essential being, you have attained dominion. When you can go to seminars, study different teachings, or participate in religious ceremonies without feeling subordinate to them or without being used to perpetuate their dogma, you are truly free. You are "in the world but not of it."

Dangerous Double-Talk

*I*n almost every teaching or book that I have come across (mine included), there is a hidden danger. In many books that otherwise have a lot of truth in them there is a contradictory double-talk of which even the well-meaning authors are most likely unaware. I became especially conscious of this when I recently plucked a book off the shelf that had greatly inspired me in the past. On re-reading it I become aware of the double-talk stumbling-blocks that I missed the first time around.

There is an important difference between double-talk and double-thinking. Double-talk is what happens when someone says one thing and contradicts it by implying something different later on, while double-think is what happens when you simultaneously see different dimensions of the same thing without confusing them. The problem with double-talk arises because it is impossible to say two things at once. At one moment someone may be talking about your unchangeable spiritual nature, but contradict it the next moment by pointing out your possible personal shortcomings. Unless it is made perfectly clear which viewpoint is being pointed out, double-talk confusion confounds the truth.

I appreciate the inspiring eloquence in most of the mystically oriented books I read that tell me that God is my true identity; however, I find that sooner or later the majority of them contradict what they have said. It is double-talk when authors tell us that we are made in the image of God and then the next minute tell us what we have to do in order to become a child of God.

It is double-talk when we are told one minute that we are all that God is, and the next minute we are told to pray to a "Him" – to something apart from our own divine reality – to make us be better than we presently are. Either we are made in the image of God at this very moment or we are not and never will be.

To avoid double-talking, I try to make it clear to others that first and foremost I recognize their divine nature as the truth of their being. Always keep advice impersonal by saying "This is what a person believes when that person is being tricked by ignorance," or something of that nature without making people feel that whatever it is is their personal fault. Next I ask them to hold that realization uppermost in their awareness while I explain to them that at those times when they see themselves as limited human beings, they are just being temporarily hypnotized.

We should never use the word "you" when speaking to someone about the ignorance of his or her essential being that they are currently expressing; our statements should always be impersonal. Do not tell a person that he or she is ignorant, or that they are other than their true selves. If we speak to them negatively it will create a crisis of perception, and that can lead to a negative self-fulfilling prophecy for them.

It is the same with your ownself. You can admit to yourself that you have made mistakes or lacked understanding, but when you do that, blame it on your temporary ignorance about who you are, rather than thinking that it *is* who you are. That's why I double-think and differentiate between Walter and the I that I AM. Walter makes mistakes. He gets hypnotized into believing he has a life apart from me, his true self. But I know that I am already all that God is – *and so are you.*

You can tell people that superimposed upon their true identity is an erroneous or limited concept of who they are, and you can do it in a way that encourages them to believe that they are divine-humans. In that way you are not encouraging them to confuse their two selves – the real self and the illusory limited self.

I am not saying that we should disregard the teachings or books that have so much valuable truth to impart to us, even though at times they may contradict themselves with double-talk. But I am saying that it is up to us to study those books and listen to those teachers with our eyes wide open. When our vision is clear we can avoid confusion and absorb what is true while simultaneously being constantly alert to contradictions that constitute double-talk.

Joel Goldsmith was speaking the truth when he wrote,

> *There is only one life, infinite life, there is only one Consciousness, infinite Consciousness, there is only one Soul, infinite Soul. The Soul of God embraces man; the Consciousness of God contains man; and the life of God is the life of man – not a part of it, but all of it. We cannot bring God to our body or mind because God is already the life of every body; every body is the temple of*

the living God. We do not have to release the kingdom
of God into the world: we only have to know that it is.

Then, without telling us that he was switching to the personal level and was addressing the truth of personal-sense rather than our divine nature, Goldsmith goes on to contradict what he has just said. He states, "You have no life of your own," and "You must die daily," though just a minute before he had said, "the life of God is the life of man – not a part of it, but all of it." The truth is that you do have a life of your own; it's your essential being, your God life. You don't have to die daily. What must die daily is not you; it is the ignorance of your true self that has to die – a false sense of self that you continue to accept because of double-talk.

It's up to us to be aware of possible contradictions that can take place when our teachers address the limitations of human nature and ask ourselves, "Which me are they talking about?" We must recognize those times when they are not talking about our essential being and avoid personally identifying with what they are saying. If we start believing that we have no lives of our own or that we must die daily, our teachers are once more encouraging us to see ourselves as sinful human beings that need to change, and that belief will become our self-fulfilling prophecy.

Until we have reached the spiritual condensate experience, we have to deal with dualistic double-talk. We can successfully do that if we double-think, and simultaneously acknowledge the difference between the nature of God or Self and the nature of error or ignorance. In order to do so we have to keep our priorities straight and always remember that we are already made in the image of God. To pray without ceasing is to banish dualism, ignorance, and contradiction by constantly realizing that we are, along with everyone else, *all that God is.*

The Sexual Giant

*I*t would be impossible to ignore an elephant if it were standing in the middle of your living room – the consciousness where you live, but that is exactly what our Western religions have tried to do with our sexuality. In the East they approach sex subjectively, while we in the West objectify it and make sex a moral issue. We haven't included the Hindu Tantric "how to's" that show us how to integrate our sexuality with our spirituality. Of all the skeletons in our guilt-filled closets, guilt about our sexual feelings and acts overshadows all the rest. Even today our sexuality is a subject most ministers or public speakers are reticent to bring out in the open. As long as sex remains such a taboo subject, and one that is primarily identified with negative exploitation, its divine purpose can't be appreciated. If we continue to separate sexuality from our humanity, and refuse to see it as an important part of our essential being, there is no way we can close the gap and understand how our humanity is an expression of our divinity.

In the eleventh century Thomas Aquinas emphasized the concept of the virgin birth in order to avoid admitting that sexuality was an integral part of Jesus' heritage. As late as 1854 Pope Pius found it necessary to remove Jesus' mother, Mary, from the taint of sex by claiming that she, too, was immaculately conceived. By refusing to connect Jesus' birth with the sex act they not only cut him off from his humanity and us from him, but they also implied that the sex act was not part of our spirituality.

When in the tenth century the Church made celibacy mandatory for priests, it was done more for monetary reasons than spiritual ones. It was the Church's intention that it appear that the order was instituted so that priests could direct their energy into serving God, but that was not the primary reason. For the first thousand years of the Christian movement priests were allowed to own land, develop wealth, and marry. Upon their deaths those priests left their estates to their wives and children who were then subject to their kings, and the church was left holding an empty bag.

I'd like to think that making the sex act a sin was not a conscious decision made by the church in order to control the people. But, in fact, the most successful way to keep people in bondage is to make them doubt the single most important motivation in their lives – love. Love expresses itself objectively as degrees of affection and ultimately as sexual intercourse. By implying that all sex acts, except for procreation, are lustful and unnatural, love itself is tainted.

Most of the time sex is defined objectively in terms of a man-made morality based on gender, legality, and performance. The time has come for us to interpret its appropriateness subjectively, in terms of the love it does or does not express. Once we expand our ability to love unconditionally, we will no longer equate sex with rivalry, fear, gender, or secrecy. We will see it as part of the process of experiencing and expanding our ability to love unconditionally.

Every human desire is ultimately a longing for divine perfection. At a subconscious, if not conscious, level we want to love, and our sexual desires represent a reaching out to the infinity and perfection that we are capable of experiencing. That is why the soul quickens in the presence of birth, either human or animal, for nowhere is the divine process of love more evident than at that time

During my seven years of monasticism I rejected my sexuality. It was not for guilt or moral reasons, but to exclude outside and physical influences. Nevertheless, I now realize that

I was denying my divinity and my wholeness. Instead of creating a feeling of unity with all life by inhibiting passion and ignoring my sexual feelings, I was playing right into the hands of self-centeredness and egotism.

Passion, expressed sexually or otherwise, is one of those energies that can as easily be used to disrupt as to create or exalt. That is why some religions advocate subduing all passion. They even imply that saints are not passionate beings, but that is absolutely untrue. Those who reach the status of sainthood do so because they care passionately. Gandhi, for instance, may have preached nonviolence, but he cared passionately about freeing his people. We don't give birth to anything of importance without passion.

Everything we do is either for the purpose of creating or destroying. The more spiritually important an activity or its energy is, the greater are the inhibitions imposed upon it. Sex tops the list because when it is an expression of love it can create life, but if it is made a moral issue its spiritual purpose is lost and it can be used to excuse or judge human excesses.

Since we do not need any more people on earth (there are enough of us now to raise the consciousness) the second purpose of sexual intercourse is for regeneration or recreation. The "re"creation of those who already exist. When the sexual act is performed out of an expression of love it heals, re-energizes, and uplifts both partners. It enhances the divine in us. Divine fulfillment is not only spiritual illumination, but according to our Christian myth it includes resurrection of the body. When the union of two people joined in love takes place, each is renewed and made divine.

Presently we are swamped with films, articles, commercials, and other types of media that are overloaded with sexual content. Unfortunately, most of it is aimed at objectifying sex and camouflages its subjective spiritual purpose. That's the downside. The upside is that this openness will eventually contribute to an undoing of centuries of sexual taboo. Though its present exploitation is degrading, by being exposed it will sooner or later lose its fascination as a guilty pleasure. As long as sexuality is kept in the closet, it will seem unnatural and we will ignore its presence as a valuable part of our essential being.

The crisis of perception relevant to sexuality will be solved once we educate ourselves to its divine purpose and realize how it is being misused. In other words, we will solve the crisis of perception when we no longer look at sexuality objectively in terms of good and evil, but think of it subjectively as love or the sharing of love as the presence of God.

The Onus of Absolutes

As I contemplated how to explain the most subtle and yet insidious cause for many of our guilt feelings, Uncle Gilbert's advice to keep it simple popped up again to haunt me. Simply put, when we believe that we can achieve absolutes at the less-than-absolute level we set ourselves up for failure.

Spiritual masters have always taught the nature of absolute truth, but by implying that we can achieve a perfect fulfillment of absolutes at the less-than-absolute human level has opened us up to a lifetime of guilt. Our theologians and teachers have taught us that our goal should be to attain perfection as human beings, but their understanding of perfection has been abstract and unattainable in the dual world where absolutes do not exist. Perfection is a subjective experience, but to expect a perfect objective result from that experience is self-defeating.

If you were to look at a thousand newly manufactured

water glasses, to your naked eye they would all look alike, but under a microscope you would see that each one was different. Which would you consider to be the perfect one? At the level of infinity everything is unique. To believe that we should absolutely be like anything or anyone else, or that we should perfectly conform to any mold, impregnates us with conscious or subconscious feelings of guilt. We can only be who we uniquely are.

When the Scripture, "Be ye perfect even as your father in heaven..." was interpreted as referring to a human or objective perfection, impossibility was born. Our father is not an object that can be perfect or not perfect. At those subjective moments when we touch Christ or father-consciousness, we could say we are perfect, but then we are not thinking of ourselves as bodies.

Absolutes do theoretically exist at a subjective and intangible dimension, and it is important for us to aim at them objectively because we will get much further, much faster, and with much less pain than we would if we did not try to achieve them, but they do not exist at the human dimension.

At the third-dimensional level of this world there are no absolutes. There is never a "never" or always an "always." We have to be constantly on guard, because such innocent sounding words as "all," "only," "always," "never," or "constantly" lays traps for us. In the books we read or the studies we follow we must be prepared to challenge the context in which absolute words are used. For example, if we believe that "We must (absolute) experience the Christ as a permanent (absolute) and continuous (absolute) dispensation," we are doomed to failure. To make progress we do need to aim toward those absolutes, but if we feel we are a failure when we do not succeed, it becomes difficult for us to pick ourselves up and try again.

I lived in Japan for a while and was surprised and pleased

when it was pointed out to me that their national art treasures always include a discrete flaw. To the Japanese, great art must include the artist's personal presence as a bridge between the human artist and his divine inspiration. They believe that by including a small flaw, an imperfect human touch, the gap between man and Buddha-consciousness is closed.

Today we hear, rightly, that "we have to get back to principle." But we have to do it in a new way, a way that shows that we value the subjective nature of a principle more than the material outcome we expect will result from following it. We have to do it without feeling guilty when appearances do not match our intent. If we can study spiritual principles in their absolute state, and at the same time double-think and aim at them as a means to an end, they are invaluable. However, if we feel guilty or at fault for not yet being absolutely able to live them, they will disconnect us from an awareness of our essential being. The only true absolute is all-inclusiveness. We are absolute when absolutely everything is included and nothing is left out – perfect or imperfect, true or false.

For years I was confused and felt that something was wrong with me, because the mystical teaching I was studying and trying to follow was full of ultimate truths; nevertheless, there was something in the teaching that made it impossible for me to fulfill what it claimed was absolutely possible. Asserting self-defeating, absolute statements like, "Once you experience the presence of God never again will you have a fear or have a worry," left me in a quandary. There were times when I felt certain that I had experienced the presence within myself, but when I once again experienced worry or fear I doubted myself, and wondered if my God experience was real or imagined. When I read, "Only those who have learned to keep their attention on spiritual things will taste joy," I thought I would never taste joy because it was impossible for me to "only" keep my attention on spiritual things all the time.

Mystics tell us that once we have touched the spirit we are never (absolute) alone and that we always (absolute) sense an inner companion. Then when we do feel alone, as Jesus did when he complained that his disciples would not stay awake with him for an hour, we have to feel that we haven't truly touched the spirit. That just plain isn't so. As long as we exist at the finite level we go in and out. An honest statement would be that as we progress we mostly never feel alone or we seldom feel as though we do not have an inner companion.

Fortunately, there is a way that we can turn half-truths into whole ones and come closer to absolutes at the less-than-absolute level. It requires an understanding of how to include complements.

Complements

*I*n the first half of this book I mentioned our need to include complements. Consciously finding and including complements is an important "how-to" achieve the benefit of absolutes at the less-than-absolute personal level.

There are two basic approaches we have pursued in our attempt to arrive at absolutes in the past. One is through subtraction, the other through addition. The first mantra I was taught when I studied Hinduism was "neti, neti," which translates into "not this, not this," the object being to subjectively eliminate everything that is not the truth in order to arrive at the absolute truth or the divine. That is a valid negative approach. It attempts to negate anything that is not God.

In the West we are taught to practice a positive and objective approach that says God includes all there is. By inclusion, rather than exclusion, we hope to arrive at the one absolute, all-inclusive God. The shortcoming of both of these approaches when practiced alone is that they encourage either-or thinking.

Today we are at the stage of our spiritual evolution where we can go beyond either-or and arrive at absolute truth at the less-than-absolute level by "both and" thinking. We do that by becoming consciously aware that everything at the finite level of this world needs a complement to make it workable. Though there are no absolutes at the personal level, when a half-truth is complemented by another half- truth, they become a whole and absolute truth. Together they are complete and effective.

Jesus knew that everything in life needs a complement. That's why his teachings include two commandments that complement each other. Both are true, but neither works without being completed by the other. The love of God is meaningless unless it is expressed as the love of others, and it's impossible to really love others unless we know what love, or God is. When two complements are integrated, together they become absolute.

In my lectures, I have often said, "You are all familiar with the statement, 'Ye shall know the truth and the truth shall make you free'." That statement alone is actually a half-truth; its complement comes from the words that precede it. The complete statement is, "If ye continue in my word, ye shall know the truth, and the truth shall make you free." The truth isn't going to make anyone free if he doesn't live it. Unless the word is lived, both the word and the way we live are meaningless.

If we want to be successful, whenever we set out to accomplish anything we have to ask ourselves what is needed to complement our goal. We must first intuit the subjective or spiritual purpose behind what we intend doing. Then we must find its complement at the objective or dualistic level of material appearances. Once we reconcile the two, we will know what to do to make our dreams come true. For instance, any successful businessman or woman knows that success is never predicated on a single decision or act. First we have to envision what we wish to achieve, and then we have to consciously think of what we have to do in order to achieve it. The way God appears at the business level is as good business principles, but that doesn't assure success unless those principles are complemented with right action.

In other words, when Scripture tells us, "In the beginning was the Word…and the Word was madeflesh," it was saying that idea complemented by action becomes realized. We will have success if we experience the consciousness of what we desire. Then, though it may take time, we must hold to that principle as a guideline while we contemplate what action is needed to complement and make our desire visible at the less-than-absolute level of human existence.

If we want to build a house, first we get a design and then we complement the design by assembling the materials and going to work. We don't start sawing up the lumber and nailing boards together without first having a complementary plan. A design without any "how to" is futile, and "how to's" without designs become chaos.

What we call grace, or fourth-dimensional consciousness, will bring opportunities into our lives and even show us what is needed to fulfill them, but then it is up to us to take action at the third-dimensional level in order to accomplish what grace has brought to us. Personal action is grace's complement. Again, this is where as humans we need to consciously double-think. At our inner absolute level we must consciously know that subjectively God, our divine consciousness, is absolutely the only power. At the same time we must be consciously aware that at the human or finite level our consciousness appears objectively as good, sound principles that we must personally act upon. *God alone won't do it.*

On the other hand, we will never be successful at anything if we do not consciously or subconsciously complement our objective goals with subjective principle. Success becomes more consistent and assured as we become consistently conscious of including complements in all we do.

Nothing

What is there to say about nothing? A lot; it is the absolute out of which all other absolutes have come, and is a necessary adjunct to experiencing the spiritual condensate and recognizing ourselves as the Third Appearance. Everything is nothing!

It is difficult to try to say something (some thing) about nothing (no thing.) Surprising as it may seem, this truth is the basis of present-day quantum physics as well as the creation story in Genesis. It includes the secret of spiritual healing and is the key to our having dominion over the world of effect.

Though Gautama the Buddha and Jesus the Christ said it in different ways, both of their teachings were based on the concept of nothingness. This father of all absolutes is what has drawn us to these masters' teachings. Because nothingness can be experienced but cannot be intellectually grasped, most of their followers missed the significance of their teachings. Those who followed Jesus made God into a supreme being, a "thing," and credited that thing with the magical power to alter appearances. They didn't see that freedom from material limitations takes place because someone, Jesus in this case, subjectively experiences the nothingness (no-thing-ness) of there being any cause in effects, in appearances. Cause is in the consciousness that creates things and not in the things themselves.

Camu and other existentialists came close to an appreciation of nothingness but didn't arrive at its spiritual implication. They realized that nothing matters, but because they didn't see consciousness as creator they ended up with an existential despair.

In Hinduism material appearances are referred to as "Maya." The implication is that Maya is an illusion. Unfortunately, the belief that appearances are illusion is itself the illusion. Those who eliminate meaning from materiality, or are unaware of its underlying spiritual nature, encourage the same futility as the existentialists. Whatever you reject rejects you in return, and when the material side of life is devalued, instead of there being abundance, healthy conditions, and material well-being, material lack and disease follow.

When Jesus said, "Don't judge by appearances. Judge righteous judgment," he was telling us that those materialistic judgments that say we are things, rather than spiritual beings or consciousness, are the lies that give false power to effects.

More recently, Mary Baker Eddy voiced the same foundation belief and healing principle that is included in Jesus' teaching by saying, "There is no life, truth, intelligence, nor substance in matter." In other words we are not dealing with things. We are dealing with consciousness, and consciousness is not a thing – it is nothing.

The absolute truth is that God as the source of creation is nothing. In order to have dominion we must believe in nothing, in "no thing" having any power over us. The power is in the consciousness that created the thing, not in the thing itself.

Omnipresence is also not a thing, and neither is

omnipotence or omniscience. *You are nothing, you are not a thing. You have an appearance that people think is you, but you are actually invisible consciousness appearing as a mental projection, a nothing.* If you turn off the projector, the projection ceases to exist. We live in an invisible world because we live in consciousness, spirit, or beingness, and those are not things. Things are results that appear at the human level as consciousness formed, but, as I keep repeating, consciousness is nothing, not a thing.

In saying that something has to be seen in order for it to exist, quantum mechanics has been repeating the same truth that Jesus and Buddha implied – *all is consciousness and that appearances are therefore nothing appearing as something.* This truth was rediscovered by the metaphysical movement a hundred-plus years ago and became its basis for spiritual healing and harmony. This is important to know because absolute principle is the only ultimate answer that is capable of solving the problems that may lead to the world's destruction.

The nature of error is nothingness claiming to be something; there is no power or truth in an erroneous appearance. If you can look right at a material appearance, without insulting your intelligence by denying that you see it, and simultaneously know that its existence is as consciousness (nothing) rather than what your eyes behold, you can take dominion. By that I mean, once we correct our error of believing that things have power, what were previously hindrances often become blessings.

When I say that we must get back to principle, I am not talking about a thought process. I am talking about getting back to a dependence on and an experience of the invisible spiritual power that brings things into manifestation – the invisible nothingness.

Our modern day prophet-scientist, Einstein, explained his reliance on the invisible nothingness by saying:

The voice of God is from within. Something within me tells me what I must do every day. Every man knows that in his work he does best and accomplishes most when he has attained a proficiency that enables him to work intuitively. That is, there are things that we come to know so well that we do not know how we know them. Perhaps we live best and do things best when we are not too conscious of how and why we do them.

Scientists are now showing us how our attitudes and our beliefs, which are not things, affect and are the cause of everything that appears in our lives. Attitudes are nothings; you can't hold one in your hand. They are invisible; however, they become visible to us in the same way that a movie is projected onto a screen. If we want to change the picture we should stop trying to change it as though it is real and, instead, change the projector that created the picture. That is how we solve the crisis of perception.

We must hear, accept, and internalize the first law of spiritual nature, which is that we are never dealing with person, place, situation, or thing, but rather with how we react to those appearances. We must resolve our problems at the level of nothingness, no-thing-ness. We can do that by impersonalizing the picture and then "nothingizing" its influence. Our job is to get to the source, the absolute principle, that which is taking place in our own consciousness. Once we arrive at the place where we no longer give power to persons, places, situations, or things by realizing that they have been created and are maintained by our own consciousness, by nothing, then we are able to erase the picture from the screen and change it to one we like better.

Recently I had what appeared to be a physical condition that became a life-affecting experience. I had gone down to Yucatan to meet with some Mayan shamans and found that I couldn't climb the pyramids because one of my legs gave me such pain. On my return to the United States an MRI was taken, revealing a swollen Achilles tendon. After a couple of months of unsuccessful therapy, the podiatrist told me that I would just have to live with the pain. His advice woke me up and started me thinking.

My body is a thing. It isn't able to respond one way or the other without consciousness animating it. By the same token, my heart hasn't the ability to beat or not beat or my hand to move if I don't tell it to. Once I took my vision off the physical situation, I once more realized that what I was having to deal with was cause, not effect. When I released the visible scene into a no-thing-ness with the realization that there wasn't any "thing" that had power over me one way or the other, freedom came and I saw the activity of my higher consciousness at work in the experience. I was led to an excellent physical trainer, and with proper exercise the pain left and I presently walk and jog a mile or more a day with my dog.

As I said earlier, absolutes are our greatest blessing and our greatest curse. *We attain our freedom by aiming at absolutes, but we imprison ourselves and create the very duality absolutes say does not exist by judging what we see as being either absolute or less than absolute. The truth is that it is nothing, not a thing, but consciousness appearing as something. Material appearances and the ills of life are nothings claiming to be something. Giving power to the illusion makes the illusion* into a something, and we *don't have to do that.*

When asked where God came from, some theologians say that God was created out of nothing. That is true because God, being consciousness, was created out of itself. Even the atom, a thing, was split by nothing – by the consciousness of a human being – an activity of spirit working through the intellect.

Because we have lived by the first law of human nature, survival based on acquiring and using things, it is still almost impossible for us to put our trust in the invisible nothing. Yet if we are to survive this current worldwide conflict, it will depend on our shifting our attention and belief away from giving power to the things that make up our objective universe. It is not a matter of blind faith. We can see that the spirit inherent in our subjective thoughts is what forms the substance and activities of our lives; therefore, to survive we must rely on spiritual principle which is subjective, immaterial, and nothing.

Dr. Herb Beierle, founder of the University of Healing in Campo, California, writes that, "Nothing new can come forth from something that is, while everything that is and ever will be flows out from the nothingness from which all is formed." He goes on to say that science is proving that the cause of everything is energy, and energy, having no substance, is not a thing, it is nothing. *Consciousness is that energy.*

Dr. Beierle makes it brilliantly simple and personal by adding, "Nothingness does not need something through which to work. Concepts are nothing. Ideas are nothing. Imagination is nothing. Illumination is nothing. Intuition is nothing. Dreams are nothing. Thoughts are nothing."

Scripture tells us to enter into our closet to pray. Our closet is that place of nothingness within each of us. You can drop all sense of things and enter that nothing that is God, the source of all that comes into being. Release your grip on objective thoughts and concepts, allow subjective reality to express itself, and spiritual wisdom will blossom. Everything that has ever been or will be comes out of the nothingness from which all has come.

Chapter 8

The Prayer Dilemma

*I*n every religion and society since recorded history, people have prayed. Whether they call it prayer or not, everyone has sought some way to receive help in times of need from something beyond their own limited resources. People wouldn't have continued to seek methods of prayer if they had not seen positive results attributed to prayer. This convinced them that it was possible for them to also avail themselves of this mysterious power. The time has come for us to become realistically aware of the source of that power and to learn how to consciously and habitually access it.

Successful prayer is what happens at those times when we are able to transcend personal sense and listen to our higher consciousness. Although my listening has become more consistent over the years, I, for one, am not confident it will always happen at the exact moment I want it to. That is one of the reasons that even thought I have spent thousands upon thousands of hours in meditation I am nevertheless reticent to comply when I am suddenly asked to pray out loud, or on cue. That is also why I feel uncomfortable and sense the presence of hypocrisy when I hear other people assume a phony, pious-sounding voice when they pray and call on God to do something, as though God could be influenced to do what God is not already doing. I do believe that holding hands around the table in a silent celebration of gratitude and a recognition of fellowship is an inspiring reminder of our oneness with each other and spirit, but asking God to bless the food as though it is not already blessed revives superstition.

For 55 years I have always set aside a time to open myself to the equivalent of what might be called praying, yet I haven't felt comfortable calling it prayer. I have seen that often the way people have been taught to pray is based on the superstitious belief that there is a personalized God somewhere who will give them what they want if they beg hard enough for it. That accomplishes exactly the opposite of what they intended. Most often when people pray they actually affirm the presence of their need and give it power rather than dispelling it. Instead of their closing the gap between themselves and their God-being, by praying amiss they widen the gap. The idea that one is praying "to" or "for" something that does not already exist creates the self-fulfilling prophecy of there being a division or separation between them or their own higher consciousness.

When people pray in order to achieve some object or condition that they desire, they do not realize that what they really want is a subjective experience. They don't really want things, but rather they want what those things represent in their lives. For instance, if someone prays for a diamond ring or an ice cream cone, he or she doesn't really want either of them. They want the feeling of pride in owning a diamond ring, or the taste and enjoyment of eating an ice cream cone. They want a subjective experience rather than the material object.

Our consciousness speaks in the language of spirit, and spirit interprets itself in terms of the fulfillment of our material needs. It is not that our higher consciousness knows our material needs and through prayer supplies them. Our higher consciousness knows nothing of our need for a new home, a computer, a healing, or a job any more than the sun knows that the plant it shines on needs its energy. However, we can experience our higher consciousness and when we do, its energy speaks to us as spirit. The spirit, in turn, manifests as our bank accounts, companionships, healings, and creative ideas.

There is a way of bringing the infinity of well-being and supply into our lives; however, it is not by repeating prayers, singing hymns, or believing that God will then give us what he has been withholding from us. The secret is that we cannot get anything that is not already in our consciousness. True prayer takes place when the conviction of "I have" is experienced.

Looking outside of ourselves for our good is what has previously separated us from that good. We have looked everywhere except where it is – within our own perceptions. Prayer is not something we do, it is an experience that takes place in, through, and as our perceptions. To pray aright is to look within our own consciousness for our good, not to an external person or source. In this new dimension you do not receive your good, but instead you perceive it. The experience of your own God-being is the source from which your good flows; that source is the Third Appearance.

Despite the fact that it has been proven that patients in hospitals who were prayed over have done far better than others who were not prayed for, it wasn't anything people thought or said that did the healing. It was not their spoken prayers that set appearances aside. What made the difference was that in the act of praying someone had an actual experience of his or her divine spiritual consciousness. It was the spiritual energy resulting from that experience that fulfilled their intent, not the words that were said or thought. A healing perception was activated by its having been experienced, and that is what produced results.

Prayers that work are the result of someone's having achieved the experience of a divine reality.

Prayer is ordinarily thought of as a noun, an objectified act or something we do. Instead, prayer is something we *are* at those moments when we are experiencing our divine consciousness. We are always praying because we are verbs and we are what we are experiencing; therefore, the power inherent in prayer is not a thought we think but rather the perception we experience and "are." If the experience is not taking place in or as us, our efforts will be fruitless.

What we must do is to strip prayer of superstition and then we will discover for ourselves what the mysterious energy is that can come through what we have previously thought of as prayer. Once we discover what that energy is and where it comes from, it can become a conscious and consistent way for us to bring harmony and healing into our lives.

I am not saying that we have to stop using the word "prayer" any more than we have to stop using the word "God," but when we use the word we must no longer think of prayer in terms of calling on God as a supreme being, a someone or something other than an experience of our own divine consciousness. In fact, whenever we sing hymns or read inspirational writings and come across the word "prayer," we will come closer to its true meaning if we can immediately think of it as "experiencing the presence of my higher consciousness." We must no longer look at prayer as something we do, but as something we experience.

The Silence

*P*rayers are experienced not by words but by the mystery of silence. When mystics old and new, East and West, speak of entering the silence, they are describing a place within themselves that is void of material sense, a place where they no longer react to past or future, a place where their prayers are experienced. If the silence were just a matter of soundlessness, anyone could experience it. One would only have to go down into a cave or enter a soundproof room. Silence is not a place; it is a distance. Silence is the vibrational or energetic distance from the turmoil of judgmental thoughts and concern into the vacuum of no-thing-ness. To enter the silence is to arrive at a tranquil nothingness where one is free from ordinary thought and opinion. It is the ability to observe the human scene without being in it. Prayer is a conditionless state of being that we can experience in meditation and devotion.

There isn't a time when I sit down to pray or meditate in order to enter the silence, that I do not come to the point where I feel that I, as Walter, don't know how to pray. If I believed that my human ego could make it happen, I would be confusing my personal sense self, my noun self, with the universal divine experiential consciousness that is my spiritual being. The best I can humanly do is to surrender to the process with trust and faith and, above all, with gratitude.

Anyone who claims to know how to pray or meditate is deluding themselves and misleading others. In its truest sense, prayer or meditation is an experience, not a set formula. We can ritualize techniques that may temporarily help us arrive at a spiritual experience, but dependence on them deprives us of the true meaning of prayer. Each one of us must find the stepping-stones that best lead us to the experience of the divine. It might be a walk in the woods, watching the sunset, listening to inspiring music, seeing a baby smile, or kneeling at an altar.

The surprisingly up-to-the-minute discourse on effective prayer or meditation called *The Cloud of Unknowing*, written by a fifteenth-century English monk, says that in trying to let go of the lower mind that separates us from an experience of our higher consciousness, the best way to pierce the cloud of unknowing is for us to beat on it with a single word. As an example, he says that if someone's house were on fire that person wouldn't call out "My house is on fire. My house is on fire." Instead, he or she would scream a single word, "Fire! Fire! Fire!" The monk suggests that if our *intent* is strong enough, our meditating on or repeating the single word "is" affirms the presence of higher consciousness and becomes a self-fulfilling prophecy - just "is," "is," "is." If we contemplate "God," "God," "God," "I," "I," "I", or "is," "is," "is" until thought centers or stops – the prayerful experience takes place within the silence.

I personally can't always move in a second from the visible world of effects, where I spend most of my time, to that inner silence. I have to sit down and perhaps read some inspiring book or my favorite Scriptures in order to stop my worldly thoughts. When something I have read resonates, I put down the book and feel what is taking place within me. As thoughts drift off, I do not resist them but rather I come back to my center by contemplating the I THAT I AM, until I sink into a no-thoughts, yet thoughtfull, state out of which inspiration comes.

It helps to realize that the silence of nothingness can be reached by any one of us if we can just let go of all of our imagined concerns and reactions. It isn't that we deny them, or that we will not deal with our problems in the future, but rather that we deal with them in a different way. We resolve them by letting go of them and entering the silence, after which we will be able to work with our difficulties on our own terms, not on theirs.

Though it can happen in a flash, experiencing the silence more often takes some time. We spend the bulk of our day at the worldly level of consciousness. That is why starting each morning with a time dedicated to opening one's self to the experience is all-important. Entering the silence is like taking a psychic bath. It cleanses our spirit and programs the rest of the day. I, personally, have the spiritual luxury of being able to spend up to and over a couple of hours each morning in meditation, but if that is not possible, even getting up a few minutes earlier than usual to meditate can make a great difference.

Remember, your *intent* is what counts. Though you may not have the amount of time you would like to have for meditation, or do not think anything is happening during your prayer time, if you set aside some time each day and keep trying , eventually the light will break through. Your inner self knows your needs and the degree of your sincerity, and when you least expect it you will feel a shift into the silence where prayer becomes effective.

Once I have experienced the silence, I do not try to force an ever deeper inner contact. I don't conjure up future concerns but rather consciously open up to whatever is at hand, large or small. I hold up whatever concerns appear for spirit guidance until their solutions are apparent. I continue to work through the litany of any remaining anxieties, shining the spirit on them one after the other until the radar screen of my life is free of any blips. At that time my so-called prayer work is over.

After concerns and judgments have been released enabling you to enter the silence, you arrive at a place where you feel that you are falling through space, and the spirit draws you into a sense of no-thing-ness by a kind of heavenly gravity. "In the moment that you think not the bridegroom cometh." It is then that you know what it means to be embraced by your divine self. The silence is pure because then, and only then, do you experience the spiritual nothingness where *all is God*.

When we take time to open ourselves to our divine consciousness without asking for anything other than the experience of that presence, what we are doing is making it possible for us to arrive at the spiritual condensate dimension where the divine and the human meet and are recognized as one. Attaining that experience is what true prayer is, and it creates the power that makes harmony and well-being appear in our lives.

One recent morning I inadvertently sidetracked myself by reading an accumulation of several days' E-mails before starting my meditation. When I finally began to meditate, my mind was buzzing with a concern about one of the messages, in particular. When I opened myself up and entered the silence, this is what I heard. "Walter, I am a jealous God. This is our time together. Keep it sacred. You don't need to ignore the thoughts and concerns that have come to you. I sent them as well, but for now take them off as you would take off a coat and put them aside. Put aside personal sense for the time being. Consciously turn to me for a while, and after we have had our communion your answers will be clear."

Once I was in the silence the spirit said to me: "Think on me. I am the peace the world knows not. I am the way, the truth, and the life. Let my thoughts be your thoughts. There is but one power and one presence in and as your life, and that is what I am, that presence. Feel me. Feel my arms wrap around you. I am peace. I am love. I am joy. I am the life you live. Be still. Let me cleanse your soul. There is no past. There is no future. Right now is all that is important, and in the moment I am all that is. I am the breath you breathe, the life you live, the love you love. Feel the world drop away, and we embrace each other as one being and one presence. Remember your promise to me, that you will turn it all over to me, and in return I will show you what to do. Sit in this communion with a smile on your face knowing that all is in divine order. See, already you have let go. Now it's your turn. Now you speak to me."

In gratitude I responded, "Thank you, my higher consciousness. Thank you for showing me how powerless my concerns have been. Thank you for the gift of forgiveness, for allowing me to release the petty concerns that have accumulated around my soul since our last conscious time together. Thank you for making me feel at home in you, the divine center within my being. Thank you for making it so simple. Thank you for surrounding me with the love that is my truth. Thank you for making it possible for me to be in the world, active, yet free of doubt and fear, or the need to feel personally responsible. Thank you for erasing any thoughts that make me feel that we are two. In you I am talking to my true being. How blessed I am! Now I will sit in the silence for a moment, and when the time is right I will address those old concerns, knowing that my guidance comes from you, my higher being."

Divine Convicts

The metaphysical movement hit the public arena with a blast over a hundred years ago, and it grew by leaps and bounds because metaphysics (mind over matter) had discovered a more powerful and less superstitious way to effectively pray than had traditional religions. By discovering that what was programmed in and sent forth through the thinking mind played an important part in the proceedings, those metaphysicians lifted prayer and spiritual healing to a new level.

It is a matter of history and record that in the early days people flocked in droves to Christian Science, Unity, and Religious Science. That wasn't accidental. With dramatic results those teachings were transforming lives, bringing about healings, and manifesting supply for the thousands who turned to them. Did those early metaphysicians have something that has diminished or been lost over the past fifty years? If the metaphysical or New Age movement has not been attracting people lately, or producing the healings that drew people to its early teachings, what went wrong?

The metaphysical movement discovered that the mind plays an important part in forming and activating perceptions, but in time many followers began to make a God out of the thinking mind and the mental work they called "treatment." They believed that thought did the healing. The mind is only a tool, like a piece of flint used to strike against a piece of metal to create a spark. The spark, the experience, is what produced the remarkable results for those early metaphysicians, and that was dependent on the conviction of those who were praying.

When words and thoughts have served their purpose, a level of conviction has to be experienced for healings to take place. Conviction is not a thought; it is an experience – a powerful energy that creates and confirms our reality. Conviction is the energy that turns thought into fact. As long as any doubt remains, conviction hasn't taken place. Those early metaphysicians were completely convinced that their prayers would succeed, and that conviction is what made it so.

In our society a convict is someone who has broken the law. For prayer to be successful we must become convicts, breaking the commonly accepted laws of disease, of lack, or of failure.

Old-fashioned prayer may not work, but it can lead to a transcendental experience via consciousness, and in that way it *does* work. The reason that a percentage of the prayers said in the past by those who were calling on God were effective wasn't because of any appeal to God. Their prayers were answered because some of those who were praying were so convinced that God would answer their prayers that they actually had a transcendental experience. It was their own conviction that did the healing, not their prayers to God.

It is no wonder that so many people today find the subject of spiritual healing repugnant. There is so much superstition , religious paraphernalia, and inconsistent results associated with spiritual healing that it is no wonder that many have shut the door on the possibility of receiving any help from other than the medical profession. It is a fact that neither doctors nor so-called healers heal people. A doctor can diagnose disease and perform the surgery that makes healing possible, but nature or consciousness does the actual healing.

Don't misunderstand me; mental process does play a part. Sometimes we have to consciously outline our desires, or the need for healing, and project them into our consciousness in order to become convinced they are being taken care of. Unless our conviction happens instantly and automatically we may need to take the time to perform what we have previously called our prayers. The purpose of thoughtful prayer is to confirm and enhance our intent, but then we must shift into the level beyond words where we become convinced that our own individual higher consciousness is at work. We are that which we experience; therefore, we are the healing. We are the miracle. When that truth turns into conviction, we enter the *now* where reality exists. Once we do that, we become inline with the divine plan for our lives and realize that we are *all* that God is. The conviction that we are the presence of God is true prayer.

In the past, we have thought that we had to receive healings from a practitioner or healer. Now we know that our own conviction that we can be healed is the experience that heals us. When Jesus said, "Your faith hath made you whole," he was talking about conviction. God, as your individual higher consciousness, is the only power. It is your confidence in that truth that heals you.

In the past we may have needed someone for us to believe in, be it a Jesus, a practitioner, or perhaps a teacher, in order for us to see that it is possible for us to have a healing consciousness ourselves. Now we can take the next step, close the gap, and peel off the next layer of the mental onion to convince ourselves that our essential being can do all things. Through conviction, we have the experience of our own divinity as our healer and our healing, even if it comes through belief in our practitioners. We may need practitioners, ministers, prayer groups, or the Silent Unity prayer service to remind us that prayer can work, but the experience of our higher consciousness is what does the healing, no matter through whom we think it comes.

Many years ago I was privileged to be among those in the home of the actor, Sir John Gielgud, in London. He was giving a party for Madam Krasavana, one of Najinski's two great ballet partners, in order for her to meet America's great choreographer, Martha Graham. Late in the evening Sir John was acting like a cross-examiner, quizzing Krasavana about the early days of the Diaghilev Ballet in which she had starred. I mentioned that the modern dancers were machine-like perfect, but that they did not excite me the way Alicia Markova, the reigning star in the late thirties had. Agreeing with me, Madam Krasavana said, "Zee modern dancers zay count, 'one, two, three, four, one, two, three four.' We learned to dance by counting and zen we forgot and danced to the music."

As a new breed of metaphysicians we may have learned the principles by counting or studying, but now it is time for us to forget counting and dance to the music. There is no magic in counting, just as there is no magic in praying with words. We have learned the letter of truth, and now we must let it go and fly.

The excitement and results that the early metaphysicians experienced will return to us, not because we will perform miracles for others, but because of the freedoms we manifest in our own lives through our conviction of the power of truth. Our lives will be examples that show others that we know the secret of successful prayer and that they can also do it for themselves. Then watch the masses knock on our doors once more.

We must dig deep within our souls for an experience of that presence, where we live and move and have our being. *If we have the slightest feeling that we are praying to a God or power apart from the experience of our own higher consciousness, we must not so much pray as surrender to a conviction of who we are – the presence of God, the Third Appearance.*

Healing Secrets

After all the other gaps are closed between the divine and the human, there is one final marriage that must take place the union of body and spirit. That takes place when we realize that the body is as important to the spirit as the spirit is to the body, and we must honor it as such.

Our tendency, particularly in the western world, is to either worship our bodies and the pleasures they can provide, or to think of them as necessary evils. The latter tendency comes from teachings that imply that our bodies represent our animal nature and must be punished or denigrated. In turn we have abused them by the unhealthy food we put into them, by the amount of alcohol we drink, by the chemicals we swallow, and by neglecting to exercise them. Rather than honoring our bodies we have been blind to their purpose and importance.

Your body houses your spirit or consciousness. In

spiritual terms, it is the temple of the living God that you are. No matter what size, shape, or condition your body is in, it is your temple and it is to be honored as such. That temple houses an invisible flame, and that flame can't exist without a temple to protect it and keep it from being extinguished. So the body really is as necessary in keeping the spirit alive as the spirit is in creating and maintaining the body. When once I finally saw the necessity of loving our bodies, I realized that the way to heal them is to recognize their divine purpose. They exist to transport, implement, and protect the sprit they house. As such, they are spirit formed. Spiritual healing depends on the spirit we experience by knowing the nature of error. Error is a lie claiming to be the truth. Error is not what is; it is what isn't currently being accepted as what is. We can't reject what isn't if we do not know what is.

We are consciousness, and consciousness is God; therefore, our bodies are temples of the living God. When the appearance of a sick body confronts us the first thing we must do is be aware of the nature or error, that what we see is not the truth of their being, then healings can start to take place. Secondly, because the body's purpose is to house the spirit, if we can experience the temple nature of the body, the appearance will then begin to transform into the likeness of that which we experience.

When Jesus said, "Enter into thy closet" to pray, he was telling us to enter our temple consciousness. We have to have a closet, a temple, to go into in order to behold the flame; otherwise, we cannot pray at all.

Healing is revealing. Healing is revealing the light in the Temple. When you can reveal the light in a temple it dispels the error, the no-thing-ness, of darkness and healing takes place.

When you feel loved it is because the person who loves you

has witnessed the truth of you – consciousness or spirit manifest as a physical presence filled with light. When someone loves you by revealing your truth, you respond to it and are healed. Your light shines more brightly because it has been revealed.

Try thinking of prayer as a kind of chemical process. Think of it as a chemical transition that takes place in your consciousness when you combine your spirit with your humanity. Sit down, convinced that you will achieve the healings or goals you ordinarily expect from prayer. If you can feel what is taking place as a kind of spiritual chemicalization, the experience can transcend the thought. If you experience consciousness as a fluid presence, or a vibrational state, and your goal is to transmute that spiritual substance into a higher vibration or spiritual energy, you can relate it to where you are and where you want to be. You can consciously let go of present thinking and spiritually *feel* yourself into what the old- timers used to call "the alpha wave state," where a sense of divine oneness with all life comes about.

I find that if I can take whatever time is needed to bit-by-bit feel myself releasing finite judgments, fears, or desires into a kind of spiritual soup, then an all-consuming sense of rightness that encompasses all our world comes about. To me, that is prayer. I am not calling on something outside of my self, but I am lifting my consciousness into its divine nature, a kind of spiritual chemicalization, where the rhythm of my life is divine. When that happens I know that my praying has been successful.

When we pray objectively, for something material such as an amount of money, we most likely won't get it. On the other hand if we pray subjectively, we will be praying to experience supply without outlining the amount, and if we contact the consciousness of supply it will meet our needs and then some. In other words, pray for anything you want as long as it is spiritual. Pray for a subjective experience and you will most likely receive whatever form is best for you – not just sufficiency but abundance.

There is a way of bringing the infinity of well-being, healing, and supply into our lives; however, that way is not through repeating prayers, affirmations, singing hymns, or believing that God will then start giving us what he has withheld from us up until now. The way is not in believing that we will get something we do not already possess, but rather the way is for us to perceive and experience the fact that we already have or include all we need within our own infinite, divine, higher spirit consciousness. The secret is that we cannot get anything that is not already in our consciousness. True mystical prayer happens when the conviction of "I have" is experienced. True prayer gets rid of past limitations by actively perceiving that *now* "I have" – not "will have" but "*now have.*"

Looking outside ourselves for our good or our healings is what separates us from our good. We have looked everywhere except where it is, within our perceptions. To pray aright is to look within our own consciousness for our good, not to a God or to someone outside ourselves. In the new dimension you do not "receive" your good, you "perceive" it. The experience of your own God-being is the source from which it flows. That is why the world is facing a crisis of perception about the meaning of spiritual healing.

There is no such thing as a spiritual healing of a physical problem. No one has ever received health as an answer to prayer. On the other hand, diseases have been healed by human intervention and lack has been replaced by abundance as the result of a spiritual experience. No, I am not contradicting what I just said. What was healed was not a disease or a lack. A perception was healed. Spiritual healing takes place when the perception of disease is replaced by perceived health.

Conditions are results, not cause. *No matter what condition appears, it is the result of formed perception.* To change the form we must change our perception of what is present. When disease is perceived as a fact it is created, not eliminated. When we resist it, we perpetuate it. So what can we do? Don't resist, *replace!* We can replace a perception of disease with one of health, and that becomes our reality.

Expecting your happiness and peace to come to you keeps them away from you. They don't come to you; they come *from your own higher consciousness.* Let peace flow from you and you will have it. The moment you experience peace as "that which I AM," you are acknowledging success and it becomes a self-fulfilling prophecy. *Experience peace within regardless of conditions without, and this will ultimately change your outside conditions.* In other words, the peace that you experience within creates harmony in your outer existence. Truth (God) is not mocked. Our prayers will succeed when we no longer perceive of our problems as problems. *In order for tomorrow to be different, tomorrow's consciousness has to be different today.*

Prayer, Grace, and the Fourth Dimension

*I*n the past we have tried to resolve our problems or anxieties by praying as though we were trying to plug up the holes in a sieve, one-by-one. Jesus warned us of that problem when he said that it is impossible to fulfill all the laws by the law since there are too many of them. However, he did propose a way that we can fulfill the aims of all the law in one swoop. If we experience the two commandments of love that he gave us we will arrive at a dimension where problems no longer exist. That dimension is known today in metaphysical and new age circles as the "fourth-dimension."

It is superstition to believe that by praying or meditating a mysterious power comes into play. There is no mystery to it. Potentially, prayer can lift one's consciousness from a third-dimensional vision of life into an experience of a fourth-dimensional awareness of life where conditions are transformed. The third-dimension is the level of time and space – when and where, good and evil. It is the level of objective vision where things matter. At that level we observe appearances in terms of what the Hindus call "the pairs of opposites," a combination of conflicting spiritual and material laws. The fourth-dimensional level is a subjective experience where we not only transcend the laws of time and space, but, without eliminating individuality, we arrive at an awareness of the spiritual nature of all being and know that because all is God there are no existing conflicts. At the fourth-dimensional level conditions no longer occupy our minds and we experience love, forgiveness, and other qualities of our divine being – not so much as fact but as a presence.

When we let go of third-dimensional thought and enter the fourth-dimension, the dimension of love, it is like placing a magnet in front of a bunch of metal filings that are laying helter-skelter. When we introduce the magnet, chaos ceases to exist, and all the elements of life line up harmoniously toward the magnet. That magnetic power is the power of love; the power that Teilhard de Chardin said was the only power capable of totalizing the world.

An understanding of what it means to go from the third-dimension into an experience of the fourth-dimension takes the mystery, but not the magic, out of the subjects of prayer and grace. Grace, like prayer, is not a mysterious power that accidentally affects our lives. It is a dimension other than the level of good and evil or of law. Grace is fourth-dimensional consciousness. When we turn our lives over to grace, we are turning them over to a life lived in and by that fourth-dimensional consciousness. At that level there is no need to ask what should or shouldn't be done, or what is good and what is bad. Decisions no longer need to be made that depend on logic. Grace is a free state of consciousness that exists beyond time and space, a place where everything is recognized as being the presence of God or higher consciousness. When we turn our lives over to grace, we are no longer personally responsible for our actions or what takes place.

When Paul wrote, "I live, but not I, Christ lives my life," what he was instinctively observing was that when he stopped taking personal responsibility and allowed his fourth-dimensional consciousness to live his life, he was at the Christ consciousness level. When Jesus said, "He performeth that which is given me to do," the "he" he was talking about was his fourth-dimensional I AM consciousness.

A master is one who lives in the fourth-dimension and perhaps even dimensions beyond that. That is what made Jesus unique. He predominantly lived out of his fourth-dimensional consciousness.

Prayer is man's attempt to let go of the objective third-dimensional viewpoint so that he can experience the higher consciousness of the fourth-dimension. Though that level of consciousness includes the personal, it sees it through the impersonal lens of universal consciousness. In order to impersonalize and experience the fourth-dimension, it is necessary to forgive or release everyone and everything from judgment. When release is completed, the belief that there is power in effect, which is third-dimensional, ceases. When the two attitudes of gratitude and release are experienced, we step into the fourth-dimension of grace where all is consciousness. The paradox is that when we do let go of our unfulfilled desires and surrender ourselves to the no-thing-ness of a life lived fourth-dimensionally by grace, all that we previously wanted and prayed for of a spiritual nature comes to us as a result of our own liberated consciousness.

The emergence of the new spiritual condensate dimension depends upon our ability to pray in a way that is effective and practical. Then if enough of us experience prayer as a fourth-dimensional experience of grace, we will no longer disenfranchise ourselves by giving away our power. As we experience the emergence of this new dimension, we will take dominion over our lives and in the process we will transform the world.

Chapter 9

To Love Life

*I*always felt guilty when I was told I should love God. When the Scriptures said that I should love God with all my heart I didn't know what it meant, so I felt I had to fake it. I thought that I was a lost soul because I didn't feel anything; therefore, I must not love God. That was partly because I equated the love of God with an emotion or a personalized desire, like loving another person. I felt there had to be a me and an object for me to love. In other words, I thought of love in terms of a personal, third-dimensional experience where I would feel something for something else. My problem came from the fact that loving God is a spiritual matter and that doesn't happen third-dimensionally. As a human being, if I wanted to know how to love God I had to transcend time and place, subject and object. Then I took it to the next step and realized that the love of God is a fourth-dimensional experience of a spiritual presence without form; so I must see loving God in that impersonal way and then I will know what it is.

No matter how many times I personally, as Walter, had read and contemplated the commandments telling me to love God and my neighbor, the utter simplicity of that commission eluded me until recently. In the past, when I tried to love an imagined God or divine principle, I drew a blank. Such an abstract concept didn't generate a warmth of soul within me, no matter how hard I tried. What finally occurred to me was the idea that if God is my life and my essential being, then *when I love my life I am loving God.* In reverse, when I am not loving my life I am not loving God.

When you look at your problems one by one you will see that they all add up to a divine process called your life. Then you can ask yourself, "Do I love my life? Will I love it more if I change it? Do I believe my life has to change in order for me to love it?" After you ask yourself those questions, you will realize that if you don't love your life just as it is at this very moment, then you are not loving God. You are not loving God because you have temporarily lost sight of, and need to redeem, a sense of your essential being. You might have to add up all the little things for which you are grateful in order to see that you do love your life. All the many things that we have to be grateful for are summed up in one phrase – "I love my life."

Once I realized that if I didn't love my life I wasn't loving God, that thought came back to haunt me. One day, when I found myself in a disturbed mood, I wondered if that meant I didn't love my life. I decided that whether I loved my life or not depended on what I meant by the word love. If I meant that I must always *enjoy* my life then I had a problem. I may not have been temporarily satisfied with conditions at the moment, but that did not mean that I didn't love the divine process of life or believe that my higher consciousness wasn't God.

It is easy for us to take offence when someone is short with us or facing us with a negative attitude, but if we can get our personal sense of self out of the way we will see that that person isn't loving his or her life, and their attack is a cry for love. When someone is disgruntled, it means that that person feels dissatisfied with life, and he or she is attacking in hopes that the response they will get in return will be loving.

At those moments when I am not loving my life, the one I am most likely to show my own negative side to is the very person that I know loves me the most. I think I do that in the hope that their love of life will placate me.

The first law of human nature is survival, andost religious teachings are based on the belief that we should rise above that law. What we must rise above is our ignorance of the underlying spiritual reason that law came into being. Our misunderstanding of the first law of human nature may fool us into believing that life depends on material things like money in the bank, protecting ourselves against our neighbors, righting wrongs, or staying healthy. But all those things mean that we want to hold on to life because we love it, and in loving it we love God. Once we realize that loving our lives depends on our trusting the invisible divine process of life that is our essential being to sustain and protect us, then we are loving God. Our desire to keep on living is our unconscious desire to love God as our lives. So when we sit down to pray the first thing we must do is to consciously love our lives just as they are, with all our hearts, with all souls, and with all our minds.

The Redeemer

Before I lecture, write, or perform any creative act, I try to consciously turn what I am doing over to my higher consciousness. To help me tune into that level of my being, I often repeat one of the prayers that remains from my early training, Psalm 19:14. " Let the words of my mouth, and the meditation of my heart, be acceptable in thy sight, O Lord, my strength, and my redeemer." Who or what am I praying to, and what is it that redeems me?

The word "redeem" comes from a Latin word meaning "to buy back." Circumstances may encourage me to believe that I must change or that I have lost sight of something I once had, but if there is truly a change or a redemption it is something that comes from within my own consciousness, not from something outside of me. Either *I make the change* or no change will happen. A whole string of experiences may graduate me into a change, but in the end it is my own consciousness that does the changing and redeems what I feel I have lost.

When the Scripture speaks about the Lord being my Redeemer, I have to remind myself who or what this Lord is. If change takes place as a result of my own consciousness, then that Lord is my own higher consciousness. It follows that when redemption takes place, when Walter buys back what he feels he has lost or is once more brought into harmony with his life, his own inner process is what does it. I AM is Walter's Redeemer, and there will be no redemption unless his I AM does it.

The words of my mouth *are the effects* that come from my consciousness. When I, as Walter, pray that the words are acceptable, I am praying that those words be in agreement with my divine or higher consciousness. When I say that the Lord is my strength, I am saying that my higher consciousness is the source of whatever power I exemplify. As a human being, I may feel that I have the strength and the power to make things happen; however, if I do it is because I am buying back my own creative source.

I might ask you, "Does the realization that there is no outside God that will do anything for you frighten you? Does it kill the magic that the belief in the existence of a mysterious God gives you?" It should not, because your own higher consciousness is as mysterious and magical as the God most people superstitiously think exists off in space.

Should you pray to your own higher consciousness for redemption? Most certainly! When your thinking mind recognizes the existence of a higher consciousness and you then request that its presence be experienced, an inner door can magically open. It will put words in your mouth that will be full of truth, and it will let your meditations come from your heart. It will redeem your human shortcomings.

Part of all of us longs for a personal God to help us in times of need. What could be more personal than our own higher consciousness? We can feel or sense its presence; we can love the fact that it is "with," "in," and "as" us, and we can be grateful for it.

Yes, let the words that come out of your mouth and the meditations that you know are bottled up in your heart be acceptable to the spirit of God that is at the center of your being. Let that spirit be your strength, and let it redeem those moments when you have fallen short of the Glory of the God that you are.

The Ritual Experience

When I began to seriously search for spiritual meaning I did it for two reasons; one was divine and the other was human. I was drawn to mystical teachings that awakened a sense of my oneness with God, and I turned my back on the church that I was brought up in because I was fed-up with double-talk and hypocrisy. In particular, I was disturbed by having to follow the church's rituals. I felt manipulated by them. I felt as though there was some power in the proceedings that would condition me to conform, and I would lose my individuality. The result was that I chose to reject all rituals.

Originally,   rituals were designed to be objective
or symbolic bridges used to initiate subjective states of
consciousness representing higher levels of spiritual awareness.
Unfortunately, somewhere along the way the original spiritual
intent was subverted, and participating in rituals was made
mandatory in order to subjugate the members of a church, a
fraternity, or an organization to its leadership. Initiates were
often told that if they did not subject themselves to certain rituals,
they would not be accepted by God, their marriages would not
be sanctified, or they would go to hell – or at the very least,
not to heaven. Required rituals became a way of intimidating
people and making them codependent on the church. In return,
churches became dependent on having members to support and
enrich them, and the result was a codependent relationship.

When the metaphysical movement came into being,
it dispensed with all rituals because of their historical misuse
butthen went to the other extreme. In my later years I found
that when some rituals were performed at random rather than
at specific times, more as a spiritual exercise than a physical rite,
they could become bridges leading us from abstract principles
to personal experiences. As long as the spiritual purpose of a
ritual is explained and experienced in consciousness, it can be a
valuable mental and physical exercise capable of closing the gap
between the divine and the human. A ritual doesn't always have
to involve other people. We can use our power of imagination
and take ourselves through a ritual in our meditation without
ever leaving home or involving anyone else. Rituals should take
place where they are most important, in our consciousness.

One Easter I participated in a program for the Edgar Cayce
Foundation at Virginia Beach. A well-known Rabbi was part of
the program, and on Saturday night he led the group through the
Passover ritual. As we ate the unleavened bread and experienced

the steps of the ritual, the Rabbi explained the meaning of each one as we were going through it. What took place wasn't just a meaningless routine ritual, it was a meaningful spiritual experience. The Passover ritual remains an important part of the Hebrew tradition precisely because the spiritual meaning of each part of the ritual is explained every time it is performed.

Several times during the past year, when I have felt that I needed a cleansing or an experience that would take me beyond unfeeling logic and help solve my crisis of perception, I have engaged myself in a ritual experience. I would either mentally create a new ritual that I could experience in meditation, or I would take myself through a reinterpreted traditional one.

There is one ritual that is central to the Christian tradition that I have found can be understood and practiced in a new, unsupestitious way. That ritual is the communion service. Once it is interpreted symbolically and is no longer taken literally, the reason for its mysterious power throughout the years becomes obvious. When I take myself through this ritual in private, and at rare times with those of my inner spiritual family, I am liberated from worldly concerns and once more am brought into an experience of myself as the Third Appearance. Once the underlying meaning of this ritual is understood and is no longer taken literally, you can see why it is the essence of the mystical experience.

Initially, the elements of the communion service were borrowed from pre-Christian pagan days, and a certain amount of that paganism has been perpetuated; however, when the meaning of communion is experienced mystically, it can lift consciousness into reality. When I took communion in my youth I didn't know what it spiritually symbolized; nevertheless, there was a mystery in the ritual that I missed in the years that followed, when I no longer partook of the ritual. Now through experiencing the communion in meditation, the mystery has come back to life for me in a meaningful way. The intent and mystery of the communion (common union) service is that when it is performed with an illumined spirit it results in an experience that closes the gap between the divine and the human and makes them One.

In sharing this ritual experience with you, I do not suggest my way as a formula for you, or that this ritual is unique. I am going to take you through it now simply to show you how this kind of experience happened to me. I do this in the hope that those who care to use their power of imagination to take themselves into an experience of their own higher consciousness will create their own rituals, and, in similar fashion, their own higher consciousness may talk to them in its own way.

To begin with, the sacraments (the sacred moments) in the communion ritual represent a celebration of Love. That is its real intent. Everyone is looking for God's love in everything he or she does. For instance, even when a man robs a bank he does so looking for God. At an unconscious level something in him says, "Through God's love it is my right to have all the riches of the world." At a subconscious level the thief is recognizing that God exists within him; he just goes about receiving the sacraments in the wrong way. But, nevertheless, when we can see the underlying purpose we will understand that behind everyone's actions is really a desire to receive and to give love.

If "God is Love," we can extend our love to the man, Jesus, because he revealed that all humans are temples housing the spirit. Our bodies are our temples. My Temple is called Walter, and inside of it is the same flame that exists in your temple. We are all in an association of temples that have the same divine flame burning within us.

We humans have the power of imagination; we can

create an image of things and bring them into physical form. Visualization precedes experience; we can use it to explore levels of consciousness in pictured terms. As long as we know that it is our own consciousness at work, we are free agents.

Come with me now if you like, and as you read these words use your power of imagination; listen to your inner spirit – there is no other power. Every so often, close your eyes and feel your inner truth before reading the next words. Know that what you feel is yourself talking to yourself.

Begin by picturing a temple that represents your most sacred place. Perhaps it's a quiet little chapel in the woods, or it may be a grand Gothic cathedral with towering arches. Create an image of your ideal personal sanctuary. See it and feel it before going further.

Now envision yourself entering your temple, your sacred body. See how you're dressed... feel what you feel as you enter this holy space...feel what your expectations are... feel what you want by entering this holy space... feel what is in your heart... feel what you are experiencing within your soul as you walk down to the altar. Do you feel any anxiety? Are you wanting the approval of spiritual authorities? Do you want to be accepted in the order? As you approach, feel the humanity of yourself that you are taking with you to the altar.

When you get to the altar, see yourself kneel before it... see your kneeling as taking your physical sense of being and honoring its spiritual nature. Now place on the altar all the baggage you have brought with you all your fears, hates, anxieties, animosities, concerns, and those places in yourself that you want to be forgiven.

Make an offering of them, knowing that what is behind the altar has the power to heal them. Give them up, release everybody, release everything, release yourself. Leave it all there at the altar. As you kneel at the altar feel that your soul is exposed and naked.

Wait a minute, and then see the priest of yourself – that loving, kind, understanding priest part of yourself that is within you. See your priest-self come and stand before you. Hear your divine inner priest say to you, "Take this bread, this wafer, and swallow it. This is the body, the consciousness, of I AM."

As you swallow the bread, realize that it's not that you are eating the body of a person; it is that when you take this consciousness within yourself, you are spiritualizing the substance of your own material body. It is not that when you eat the bread, you are becoming something that you have not been. You are becoming aware of something that you ARE – *a spiritual being with a spiritual body.*

As you eat the bread, see that the very substance of your body is spiritual substance. And when you take into yourself the consciousness that Jesus had, that all the saints and masters have had, see yourself swallowing that consciousness… see your body becoming sanctified. Your body is in communion with the spirit.

And then the priest of you comes to you with loving compassion, holds out the golden chalice with the wine and says, "Here, drink, this is my blood." What is the blood? It is the spirit that pours through your whole body, so the consciousness of the Christ that you have swallowed and the spirit of love that flows through you complement each other. And when the consciousness and the spirit have entered your body, you recognize the divine self that you are: whole, pure, and complete.

As the spirit flows through your body, feel it cleansing you of all that you have thought were your shortcomings, of all your fears, all your anxieties, all your concerns, and all the concerns you have had for others. Know that because your loved ones are part of you, they, too, are included in this communion. All that is in your consciousness is purified. You are purified. You are free; the past has been washed away. You are re-born, pristine and whole, without any blemishes.

And then the priest of you says,

Do this in remembrance of me - the I AM that I AM... I, I, I,...I AM that which you are... You are all that I AM. I AM the only and the total truth of your being, physical being, emotional being, mental being, spiritual being. It is I... I is the name of God... I is your Name. I...I...I. Every step you have taken in life has been leading you to me, the true essence of your being. You have not chosen me; I have chosen you... I will fulfill you until the end of time... I know that the world has told you otherwise, but dare to believe, dare to believe that you are the living presence... I AM the living presence.

Say it to yourself... I...I...I. I AM THAT I AM... I AM THE WAY, I AM THE TRUTH, I AM THE LIFE, I AM THE LOVE... This is what I AM. I AM THAT I AM.

Though you may at times make your bed in hell, I AM there because there's no place that you can go where I AM not. I...I...I AM appearing as your body-temple. I AM appearing as your mind. I AM appearing as your spirit... There is only one, and I AM that one... At this moment there is no separation between body and spirit because I AM both. As you recognize that I AM, it is like a flower, a bud, opening up showing its petals, the thousand-petal lotus, revealing all the infinite nature of that which I AM... Oh, fear not! Fear not - you have seen and you will never forget... It is I. I AM the healing. Be still and know that I AM. Be still. In quietness and in confidence is your strength. I...I...I.

This one presence is you. This one presence is that which I AM, embodied in all these forms, infinite forms. Infinity is expressing itself as your being... I AM expressing myself as everybody and every presence – as everything.

Fear not, the light won't go out, it can't go out. Once it is lit, it stays lit. You can turn to it at any time that you go into your temple, for there it burns eternally.... A single flame, the I that I AM.

I have no problems. So when I turn to the I THAT I AM, there are no problems.

I AM your shepherd - you shall not want. I have made you to lie down in abundance. I have led you beside the still waters of inner peace... I have restored my presence within you... I lead you in the paths of righteousness for my name's sake. I...I...I. Yea, though you walk through the valley of the shadow of fear, I AM your being... My truth is your rod and staff. I prepare a table before you in the presence of ignorance... I anoint your thoughts with the spirit of love... Surely goodness and mercy will follow you through your life, and you will dwell in the consciousness of that which I AM forever.

All is healed, all is revealed... I AM, and I always have been... and always will be. And at every step that you have taken I have been there - leading you into it and leading you through it, and all of it leading you to me - the I THAT I AM...

Rest... Rest in the I.

Now when you enter the temple, you are home. You're at home in this body because that's where I AM... And the Light that shines from this I that I AM is grace. Wherever this Light touches, there is Love, there is healing, and there is beauty... Beauty is in the "I" of the beholder...Gratitude is the recognition that I AM the grace, and every time you feel gratitude, you are honoring me, the I AM of your being...I am your gift to yourself. And I am Love.

Now, dear one, return to your everyday consciousness knowing as never before that all the past is gone. You are cleansed. You are the light of the world. It is done. Be grateful for having your body temple because now you know the secret that inside of this Temple I AM, and I AM life and I AM love.

Thank you. Thank you for having a temple to protect me, the I AM, from ignorance. Come back into the world knowing that your name is writ in heaven, and say 'Thank you Father, Thank you, Thank you, Thank you.'" And so it is.

* * * *

*Thank you for spending this time
with me.
I AM*

About the Author

Walter Starcke, a fifth-generation Texan, graduated from Trinity University in San Antonio and served as a Naval Officer in the Second World War. After the war he went to New York, where he had a very successful career in the theater. In 1951, at age 31, he became the youngest producer to ever win the coveted Drama Critics Award for producing the play I Am A Camera, which later became the musical Cabaret.

Starcke studied all the major world religions, spending time at the Vedanta monastery in Southern California when Aldus Huxley, Christopher Isherwood, John van Druten and others were pursuing the perennial philosophy. For eighteen years he traveled extensively with the Christian mystic, Joel S. Goldsmith, who became his most significant mentor.

Retiring from the theater in 1960 to dedicate his life to his search for spiritual meaning, he moved to Key West, Florida where he started a highly successful business venture that became nationally famous. During that time he was named Citizen of the Year for Key West.

In the years following his life in Key West, Starcke traveled around the world five times, spending time in Zen and other monasteries, visiting Lama Govinda at the border of Tibet, and becoming acquainted with many world spiritual leaders. In 1967 Harper and Row published his first book, The Double Thread, and followed with several others. Starcke started his own publishing company the Guadalupe Press in 1987.

Starcke has been honored with a Doctor of Divinity degree from the Emerson Theological Institute. And in 2000 the International New Thought Alliance awarded Starcke the "Mystic Century Award."

Starcke now lives on his ranch outside of San Antonio, Texas where he continues to study and write. He still lectures extensively, both in the United States and abroad.

FASSI
The Foundation for the Advancement of
Spiritual and Secular Integration

The reconciliation of the human and the divine is a theme that runs through all of Walter Starcke's writings and lectures. With that goal in mind, in the late twentieth century the Foundation of the Advancement of Spiritual and Secular Integration (FASSI), was established as a nonprofit foundation.

FASSI purpose is to encourage unity and eliminate the either-or way of looking at life that has perpetuated division in all walks of life – spiritual, physical, social, and governmental. Its funds are used to produce and mail a newsletter, create programs that foster various aspects of the integration of the divine with the human, present workshops based on expressing the divine in the arts, sponsor scholarships to seminars and retreats, and in contributing to other organizations with the same goals.

Contributions are tax-deductible.
For correspondence or newsletter requests, contact:
FASSI
P.O. Box 865
Boerne, Texas 78006